Counseling Programs

The Program Evaluation Guides for Schools
Richard M. Jaeger, Series Editor

Evaluating School Programs: An Educator's Guide
  James R. Sanders

Special Education Programs: A Guide to Evaluation
  Ada L. Vallecorsa, Laurie U. deBettencourt, Elizabeth Garriss

Counseling Programs: A Guide to Evaluation
  L. DiAnne Borders, Sandra M. Drury

Reading and Language Arts Programs: A Guide to Evaluation
  Mary W. Olson, Samuel D. Miller

Programs for At-Risk Students: A Guide to Evlauation
  Rita G. O'Sullivan, Cheryl V. Tennant

Mathematics Programs: A Guide to Evaluation
  George W. Bright, A. Edward Uprichard, Janice H. Jetton

L. DiAnne Borders
Sandra M. Drury

Counseling Programs

A Guide to Evaluation

The Program Evaluation Guides for Schools
Series Editor: Richard M. Jaeger

CORWIN PRESS, INC.
A Sage Publications Company
Newbury Park, California 91320

Copyright © 1992 by Corwin Press, Inc.

All rights reserved. No part of this book may be reproduced or utilized in any form or by any means, electronic or mechanical, including photocopying, recording, or by any information storage and retrieval system, without permission in writing from the publisher.

For information address:

Corwin Press, Inc.
A Sage Publications Company
2455 Teller Road
Newbury Park, California 91320

SAGE Publications Ltd.
6 Bonhill Street
London EC2A 4PU
United Kingdom

SAGE Publications India Pvt. Ltd.
M-32 Market
Greater Kailash I
New Delhi 110 048 India

Printed in the United States of America

Library of Congress Cataloging-in-Publication Data

Borders, L. DiAnne (Leslie DiAnne), 1950-
   Counseling programs : a guide to evaluation / L. DiAnne Borders, Sandra M. Drury.
      p.   cm.   —(Essential tools for educators)
   Includes bibliographical references and index.
   ISBN 0-8039-6036-0
   1. Educational counseling—United States—Evaluation. I. Drury, Sandra M. II. Title III. Series.
LB1027.5.B64 1992
371.4'0973—dc20   92-30714
                                                                     CIP

The paper in this book meets the specifications for permanence of the American National Standards Institute and the National Association of State Textbook Administrators.

92 93 94 95 10 9 8 7 6 5 4 3 2 1

Corwin Press Production Editor: Tara S. Mead

Contents

Series Editor's Preface   vii

About the Authors   ix

Introduction   1

Vignette One Determining Students' Preferences for Small Groups   11

Vignette Two Evaluating Individual Counseling Services   20

Vignette Three Using Control Groups in Program Evaluation   30

Vignette Four Evaluating Classroom Guidance   43

Vignette Five Assessing Parents' Opinions of the Overall Program   53

Vignette Six Surveying Teachers' Opinions of Selected Program Components   67

Conclusion   77

About the Resources   79

Resource A: Standards and Indicators for the Evaluation of School Counseling Programs With Suggested Evaluation Methods and Key to Vignettes   81

Resource B: Selected References on Program Evaluation   89

Index   93

Series Editor's Preface

Essential Tools for Educators: The Program Evaluation Guides for Schools is a series grounded in the premise that regular evaluation of school programs can be of enormous help to school professionals—provided *they* are the ones who plan the evaluations, conduct the evaluations, and use the evaluations to guide their school improvement activities. Evaluation is a powerful tool for documenting school needs, identifying strengths and weaknesses in school programs, and discovering how to improve almost every aspect of school life. Program evaluation need not be complex or inordinately time-consuming. Simple principles and strategies are described in the initial volume of this series, *Evaluating School Programs: An Educator's Guide*. Then, specific techniques and approaches are illustrated in the program-focused guides that complete the series. Using these principles and techniques, teachers, principals, and other school professionals *can* plan, conduct, and interpret the findings of powerful evaluations of their curricula; of their instructional programs in mathematics, reading, language arts, and special education; of their programs for "at-risk" students; and of their counseling and personnel development programs. The principles to be learned from this series can be applied even more broadly to the evaluation of school disciplinary programs, student assessment programs, community relations programs, and other programmatic elements that are central to the successful functioning of a school.

Extensive technical training is *not* prerequisite to planning and conducting sound evaluations of school programs. Sound evaluation *does* require a desire to improve one's school, willingness to work collegially, careful attention to detail, and basic knowledge of how school program evaluations should be carried out. The ETE series provides school professionals with the last of these elements—the essential tools they need to plan and conduct effective evaluations of their school programs.

Evaluating School Programs: An Educator's Guide is the foundation volume in this series. It contains a clear, concise exposition of the objectives, principles, and core issues that undergird solid evaluations of school programs. By reading this guide, teachers, principals, and their colleagues will learn how to (a) determine the feasibility of conducting a school program evaluation, (b) focus a school program evaluation, (c) structure and design a school program evaluation, (d) conduct a school program evaluation, (e) interpret the results of a school program evaluation, (f) report and make use of the results of a school program evaluation, and (g) ensure that a school program evaluation is conducted ethically, damages no one, and enriches all who are associated with the program being evaluated.

Once these basic elements of a school evaluation are well understood, readers will be ready to proceed to the guide in this series that focuses on the subject area of the program to be evaluated. Each program-specific guide provides specific instruction on the evaluation of school programs in a single subject area, and each follows a consistent pattern of organization. Following an introduction that provides an overview and rationale for program evaluation in its subject area, each program-specific guide contains a sequence of vignettes (chapters) that illustrate, in detail, evaluation of a focused aspect of a school program. Collectively, these vignettes illustrate how evaluations of school programs are planned, structured, staffed, conducted, interpreted, and used. The vignettes cover a wide range of practical evaluative issues; illustrate the selection, development, and use of a large number of evaluation strategies and instruments; and show how the results of evaluation can be used to strengthen school programs. Resources at the end of each program-specific guide contain a set of research-based standards and indicators of school program quality, a road map to the use of these standards in evaluating the effectiveness and efficiency of a school program, and an annotated bibliography of selected references on program evaluation in the subject area of the guide.

Evaluations can help school professionals make their school the best it can be and, in the process, substantially increase their own educational effectiveness. In the hands of thoughtful, well-trained school professionals, evaluation can be a transformative catalyst that improves schools and all who work and learn in them. The ETE series will help you become one of those distinctive school professionals who can make school program evaluations work well. Knowing that your investment in this knowledge will pay rich dividends for years to come, I wish you every success.

RICHARD M. JAEGER
University of North Carolina,
Greensboro

About the Authors

L. DiAnne Borders is an Associate Professor of Counselor Education at the University of North Carolina at Greensboro, where she teaches and supervises students in school, community, and college university counseling courses. She has worked with school counseling professionals in a variety of school systems in the United States and Lima, Peru, consulting with them on issues such as program evaluation, clinical supervision, and parental involvement. In this work, and in this book, she has drawn on her experience as a teacher and counselor in public and private schools. Her numerous publications reflect her extensive research program in counseling supervision. These publications include studies of existing and preferred supervision practices for school counselors and other counseling practitioners, a comprehensive review of the school counseling literature, and investigations of counselor development and supervisor training. She also is coauthor of the *Handbook of Counseling Supervision* and coeditor of a *School Counselor* special issue concerned with innovative approaches to professional development for school counselors. She has received several awards for her writing and research. Her professional service activities include serving as co-chair of the American Association for Counseling and Development's Ethics Committee, chair of the Association for Counselor Education and Supervision's Supervision Interest Network, and editorial consultant for five professional counseling journals. She completed her Ph.D. in counselor education at the University of Florida, her M.Ed. in counseling at Wake Forest University, and her B.A. in English at the University of North Carolina at Greensboro. She has one son, Jacob.

Sandra M. Drury received her B.A. in psychology from the University of Hawaii at Manoa. While at the University of Hawaii, she served as research assistant in program development within the Kamehameha Early Education Program (KEEP). Her experience at KEEP convinced her that when teaching and learning are symbiotic, both are elevated in quality. She combined dual interests in psychology and education at the University of North Carolina at Greensboro, where she earned her M.Ed. and was awarded North Carolina certification in school counseling for grades K-12. Her work with L. DiAnne Borders enabled her to apply her research and evaluation experience to the field of school counseling. She believes that individual school counseling programs can and must dramatically shape their school's ecology, facilitating an environment and culture in which learning is optimal. Through program evaluation, she hopes that school counseling programs can rise to such a role. She has been associated with a human services agency that enabled her to consult and counsel within the public schools through the agency's outreach counseling program. Currently, she is living in the mountains of North Carolina, where she works in the Family Preservation Project within the New River Mental Health system. A large piece of her work continues to be consulting with public school personnel and counseling children with behavioral and academic problems.

Introduction

Scenario 1

The state legislature is debating a bill that would mandate school counselors for all public elementary schools and provide funding for those counselors. You are an elementary counselor in a system that uses local funds to provide a counselor in each elementary school. In your local newspaper, you read the following quote from your state representative:

> I have yet to get a satisfactory answer concerning the purpose of having a counselor in an elementary school, much less any evidence that they make a difference. Elementary school students don't need help with a college application or financial aid, like high school students do. And I can't believe it takes a master's degree to register children and assign them to classes. I just can't justify spending this much money to make kids "feel good."

You decide to organize the school counselors in your system to educate your representative and lobby for the bill. An important component of this campaign will be concrete evidence of the impact of school counseling programs in elementary schools. Results from local schools (as compared to results from other states or those reported in the literature) will be critical.

Scenario 2

Your school has the highest percentage of at-risk students in the state, but it is allocated counselors based on the statewide counselor:student ratio. Your requests for additional counselors have been unsuccessful; there is no local or state money available. Last year you attended a workshop on special programs for at-risk students, and this year you've managed to fit several of the suggested interventions into your schedule. The students you've seen seem to be benefiting from your interventions, and you are eager to expand the program.

You learn of a funding source for special programs targeting at-risk students and decide to apply. The grant application must include a statement of need, a description of the proposed program, and evidence of a pilot project conducted by the person requesting funding. To have a chance for funding, you need to document your success this year.

Scenario 3

For several years, you have offered small groups at your school that have focused on the most critical needs of students. You have routinely collected evidence that your small groups are effective, and you would like to offer more, but there's just no time in your schedule. An eager intern provides the opportunity to add two or three new groups this semester. The two of you have created a list of 10 topics for these additional groups, but you aren't sure which to offer.

Scenario 4

You instituted a new comprehensive career development program at your high school last year. Student evaluations of various aspects of the program (e.g., classroom guidance units on career exploration techniques and decision-making skills, small groups focused on résumé writing and job interviewing, individual testing) were quite positive. This morning you received the results of standardized assessments of students' knowledge and skills in career development. Overall, students' scores were above the national average except in one area: decision making. You call a meeting to discuss these results with the other counselors and to explore what changes may be necessary in the decision-making modules of the career development program.

Why Evaluate the School Counseling Program?

Each of the above scenarios points to a rationale for conducting program evaluation. Yet, as the scenarios illustrate, too often the need for evaluation results becomes clear too late in the game. For example, the counselors' lobbying campaign in Scenario 1 will be severely crippled unless they have been evaluating their programs on an ongoing basis and have evidence to present.

Introduction

Ongoing evaluations of school counseling programs can be useful in many situations. In general, evaluations are conducted for three reasons, which are detailed below.

Needs Assessment

As illustrated in Scenarios 2 and 3, needs assessments are used to secure information on program contexts. Needs assessments would be conducted to answer questions such as the following:

- What are students' needs for counseling services? Which needs should be given priority? How have students' needs changed over the last few years?
- What kinds of support do teachers need (e.g., consultation about individual students, skills for conducting effective parent conferences)?
- What are the needs of parents (e.g., workshops on parenting skills or applying for financial aid, individual and/or family counseling sessions)?

Formative Evaluation

Formative evaluations are conducted as a program unfolds. They are designed to identify strengths and weaknesses of a program. On the basis of such evaluations, changes can be made as a program is being implemented. Scenario 4 portrays a situation that calls for this type of evaluation. Formative evaluations would be conducted to answer questions such as the following:

- Who are the recipients of school counseling services? Do the "intended audiences" receive services designed for them?
- How well are various program components working? What aspects of the program need to be improved?
- What are the short-term outcomes or effects of the counseling program? Do students (or parents or teachers) gain the knowledge, skills, or self-awareness intended?

Summative Evaluation

Summative evaluations are conducted at the completion of a program and provide information about overall effectiveness. Scenario 1 is a situation that calls for this type of evaluation. Summative evaluations would be conducted to answer questions such as the following:

- Which aspects or components of the current school counseling program should be continued?
- Which aspects or components should be replaced?

In brief, counselors should conduct program evaluations to identify needs (and thereby establish goals) and to determine program effectiveness (i.e., what works *and* what needs to be changed). Beyond the impact on local decisions, evaluation results may have far-reaching effects in terms of legislation, resources, and public relations. (For a more complete discussion of the three reasons for conducting evaluations, see Chapter 1 of *Evaluating School Programs: An Educator's Guide,* the general guide for this series.)

Assumptions Underlying This Guide

What Is the Purpose of This Guide?

An important assumption underlying this guide is that school counselors *can* conduct effective evaluations of their programs. Evaluations need not involve sophisticated statistical procedures and fancy research techniques. Care in planning, organizing, and conducting evaluations is necessary, but advanced courses in research design and statistics are not prerequisites for valid and useful evaluations. We firmly believe that, given the opportunity and time to read this guide and the accompanying general guide, school counselors can develop the knowledge and skills to conduct useful evaluations. Thus this guide (as with all of the guides in this series) is meant for practitioners rather than professional evaluators.

Another assumption underlying this guide is that evaluation can be *proactive* rather than reactive. School counselors can evaluate their programs on their own terms and for their own purposes rather than those imposed by others. School counselors can use evaluations to improve the quality of their programs, determine the effectiveness of specific program components, and identify strengths and areas needing improvement. In addition, they can document resources necessary for program improvement. In effect, program evaluations can help school counselors become convincing advocates for their services and, in effect, improve their professional lives.

The Program Evaluation Guide Series

This guide is part of a series on evaluating the spectrum of programs, services, and personnel found in today's K-12 schools. The general introductory guide describes the steps involved in conducting an evaluation, including ways to focus the evaluation, identify specific evaluation questions, collect information, and then organize, analyze, and report the information. A final chapter of the general guide is focused on the logistics, politics, and ethics of program evaluation.

Introduction

This guide (and the companion guides for evaluating programs in reading, math, special education, etc.) illustrates and shows how to apply the steps presented in the general guide; in-depth explanations of evaluation procedures are not repeated here. Readers are encouraged to consult the general guide before beginning plans for an evaluation of a school counseling program.

How This Guide Was Created

The first step in preparing this guide was a comprehensive review of the literature on effective school counseling programs. This literature review (Borders & Drury, 1992; see "About the Resources", pp. 79-80) was then used to create the list of characteristics of effective programs that appears in Resource A. This list can serve as a framework for thinking about your program and as a guide for determining which components of your program should be evaluated.

How This Guide Is Organized

The guide consists of a series of vignettes containing miniature case studies. Each vignette illustrates an evaluation from start to finish and is based on one of the indicators of the quality of school counseling programs listed in Resource A. In each vignette, we describe the school setting and the purpose for evaluating some aspect of a school counseling program. We then describe counselors' deliberations about choosing an approach that will provide valid information that is related directly to the purpose. In some vignettes, counselors create needed instruments, including survey questionnaires, checklists, and interview protocols. Data collection, analysis, and interpretation (application of the results) are illustrated, and implications for the school counseling program are discussed. We conclude with a summary list of the evaluation principles illustrated in the vignette, other evaluation strategies that could have been used, and some precautions regarding misinterpretation of the results.

Indicators of Quality

In preparing this guide, we wanted to illustrate evaluations of a variety of indicators of program quality, but we could not include them all. We made several decisions regarding which indicators in Resource A would serve as the foci of our detailed evaluation vignettes. First, we eliminated indicators that could be assessed by inspecting existing records, documents, or facilities (e.g., Indicators 1.1, 4.3, and 10.2) or that could be assessed by tallying logs kept by counselors (e.g., Indicators 7.7 and 7.12). Instead, we decided to focus on indicators that required greater planning and background work, as well as those that offered the greatest potential for helping school counselors answer frequent questions about program effectiveness (i.e., Standards 8 and 9; see Resource A). Subsequent decisions about what to include in each vignette were based on our goals of illustrating a variety of instruments, data collection procedures, and methods for organizing, analyzing, and reporting evaluation results. Finally, we included examples based on elementary, middle, and high school counseling programs. Other examples of program evaluations can be found in the books and articles described in the bibliography in Resource B.

How Do I Use This Guide?

Steps in Using This Guide

As previously suggested, readers are encouraged to read the general guide first and then skim this program-specific guide to get an overview of its contents. Once the reader is ready to begin working on an evaluation plan, the sequence of actions detailed below is suggested.

Focusing the Evaluation

Evaluations don't happen in a vacuum. Instead, a program evaluation is intentional, conducted for a particular purpose or to answer specific questions, such as those illustrated in the preceding scenarios. Thoughtful planning is needed to focus an evaluation of a school counseling program so that the results will provide information relevant to the purpose of the evaluation. The list of indicators in Resource A can provide ideas and materials to stimulate and focus discussion concerning the planned evaluation; the questions below can help counselors focus or decide what to evaluate. (See Chapter 2 in the general guide for more information on focusing evaluations.)

Why Is the School Counseling Program Being Evaluated?

The *purpose* of the evaluation influences several aspects of the plan, including whether it takes the form of a needs assessment, formative evaluation, or summative evaluation. Some specifics related to purpose include the following:

- Is the evaluation being conducted for your own reasons, or are you responding to a request from someone else?
- Who will see and/or use the evaluation results?
- What will you and/or the others do with the results?
- What decisions will be based on the results?
- What actions might occur based on the results?

Introduction

Which Parts of the School Counseling Program Should Be Evaluated?

This question is related to purpose. Which program components are most relevant to the intended decisions or actions? What standards or indicators are most critical to the decisions or actions? The intention of the evaluation—decisions or actions that will be based on evaluation results—help to identify which program components are to be evaluated.

The focus of the program evaluation also may be based on the goals and priorities for a particular time period. For example, if program interventions for at-risk students are a priority this year, counselors probably would concentrate on evaluating these interventions.

A comprehensive evaluation plan also can provide answers to the question of evaluation focus. Such a plan helps ensure a systematic approach, so that each program component is evaluated on a regular basis and an overall evaluation of the school counseling program is conducted every few years (see Indicators 8.1 through 8.6).

What Resources Are Available?

Resources include persons who can serve as members of an evaluation team or as consultants, plus the time and money that can be devoted to the evaluation. Who can work on the evaluation? Are funds available for supplies and materials? For secretarial services?

For various reasons (illustrated in the following vignettes), counselors themselves sometimes cannot complete all the steps in an evaluation. For example, counselors asking students in face-to-face interviews whether the counselors were effective probably would not produce valid information; outside evaluators would be required. In addition, evaluation can be quite time-consuming, and large projects may require some specialized skills; an outside consultant and/or evaluation team might well be needed if all aspects of a school counseling program were to be evaluated at the same time. Counselors may solicit help with designing data collection instruments, producing and distributing them, and/or tallying and analyzing the results. The scope of an evaluation will depend on available resources.

Collecting Information

Now the task is (a) to determine what information is needed to answer the questions that have been identified, and (b) to specify alternative ways to gather that information. In each of the vignettes, counselors consider several approaches to collecting data; advantages and disadvantages of each are included. This information will help you choose whether to administer a questionnaire, conduct interviews, or use some other data collection strategy. It also will help you determine whether to survey all or a random sample of a group (e.g., students, teachers, parents). In addition, alternative approaches are discussed in a separate section following each vignette.

Resource A also may be helpful here. The last column in Resource A indicates which vignette(s) illustrates the evaluation methods suggested for each indicator. Reviewing the referenced vignette may be helpful in selecting an evaluation method and making plans for implementing the method. (See Chapter 3 in the general guide for a further discussion of collecting information.)

Specific questions relevant to the task of collecting information include the following:

- Who will work on the evaluation? One person? An evaluation team?
- Who will be the evaluation leader?
- How long will it take to collect the information? To analyze the information?
- When are the results needed?

Organizing the Evaluation

As most school counselors realize, an organized program—and program evaluation—increases efficiency and effectiveness. A helpful resource for organizing an evaluation plan is the construction of a time line that specifies each action step, the person(s) responsible for each task, and beginning and ending dates for accomplishing that task. It is wise to keep careful check of the information as it comes in, so that there are opportunities to correct or clarify the information and locate missing information. (See chapters 3 and 4 in the general guide for more on organizing information.)

Specific questions relevant to organizing a program evaluation include the following:

- What data collection procedures will be used? When will they be used?
- Who will collect data? Do these persons need to be trained?
- If instruments (e.g., survey questionnaires, checklists) are to be used, how will respondents be selected?
- How will confidentiality be maintained? Is informed consent needed?

Analyzing the Information

To understand what evaluative information means, the data need to be summarized and analyzed. Depending on the type of information that was collected, the summary may take the form of a verbal narrative or a statistical summary that includes, for example, frequency distributions (graphs or charts), average scores (means, medians, or modes), and/or measures of the variance of scores (e.g., range, standard deviation). Various approaches to summarizing data are illustrated in the vignettes. School counselors will need to determine who will tabulate and/or analyze the data once they are collected and to consider whether or not these persons will need to be trained. (See Chapter 4 in the general guide for a discussion of analyzing information.)

Reporting the Results

Some evaluations of school counseling programs will require the preparation of a formal written evaluation report; others will not. Whether or not a formal written report is required depends largely on the purposes of the evaluation and the audience for the evaluation. If an evaluation of a school counseling program is strictly formative and the audience consists solely of a school's counselors and principal, a formal written report might not be needed. Even so, a clear, written record of the steps used to conduct the evaluation and a written summary of what was found should be prepared in case the evaluation is later used for other purposes, and so that later generations of counselors at the school can learn what was done and what was found.

If you were using an evaluation of your school counseling program to influence a state legislature (such as in Scenario 1) or to seek additional resources from a school board, an oral report and a written executive summary of the evaluation probably would be needed. The executive summary would describe the results of the evaluation and provide an interpretation of those results (decision makers like to see the "bottom line" first), the purposes of the evaluation, and the methods used in conducting the evaluation (to support the credibility of the evaluation).

If you were using an evaluation to support a proposal for funding that was submitted to an outside agency, you would want to include an executive summary and, in most cases, a formal written evaluation report that provided greater detail on the design, implementation, and results of the evaluation. (See Chapter 5 in the general guide for more information on reporting evaluation results.)

A Step-by-Step Plan

By following the above sequence, a *step-by-step evaluation plan* can be written. Such a plan identifies what is evaluated, who evaluates, and when and where the evaluation will take place. The plan consists of a time line, resources, step-by-step procedures, and plans for reporting the results. Although creating a detailed evaluation plan takes time, it actually saves time in the long run. With a plan, you are organized and well prepared. You also avoid the frustration of having conducted an evaluation that does not provide relevant or valid information.

Summary

In this introduction we have presented several reasons for conducting evaluations of school counseling programs, outlined the general steps or stages in conducting an evaluation of a school counseling program, and given you an overview of the content of this guide. In the following sections, the points presented in this introduction are illustrated in a series of vignettes that portray evaluations of important elements of school counseling programs. Sources listed in the bibliography (Resource B) at the end of this guide provide additional examples.

1

Vignette One

Determining Students' Preferences for Small Groups

Crest Middle School serves a rural county in southeastern Texas. Although the area is made up primarily of family farms and small towns, a large army base also is located in the county. Because of the army base, the 450 students in grades 6-8 at Crest are a diverse population, representing a variety of racial and ethnic groups as well as being diverse in their geographical origin. In addition, there is a 50% turnover in the student population each year.

Focusing the Evaluation

The two counselors at Crest, Ms. Betts and Ms. Healy, are well aware of the unique challenges presented by their student population. There are constant demands for enrolling new students, orienting them to the school, and responding to their adjustment problems. The counselors also are involved in classroom guidance, frequently consult with teachers and parents, and regularly deal with the typical crisis situations of middle school students. As a result of previous evaluations by the principal and teachers, Ms. Betts and Ms. Healy know they are seen as important support staff for the school. They sometimes feel, however, that they spend the majority of their time in a reactive rather than a proactive stance, and they wonder how many of the students are aware of their varied counseling services. To change their reactive emphasis, they would like to offer a variety of small groups focused on developmental and topical issues.

In planning for the upcoming year, Ms. Betts and Ms. Healy set two goals: (a) to inform all students of their counseling services, and (b) to increase the number of small groups offered throughout the year. They generated a list of possible topics for small groups, but they weren't sure which to offer first. They also wondered if students in each grade level might need different groups. Reviewing the list of standards and indicators for school counseling programs during a brainstorming session, they identified their first step: a needs assessment.

> *Indicator 8.5.* Needs assessments of students, parents, teachers, and other school personnel are conducted regularly as a means of identifying local priority needs.

Choosing the Source of Information

Strategy for Collecting Information

The counselors first considered from which group(s)—students, parents, teachers, or other school personnel—they would gather information for the needs assessment. They believed that parents would be aware of their children's general needs but might provide fewer answers about school-specific issues. Teachers certainly would be aware of students' needs, and surveying or interviewing the 24 teachers at Crest could be a relatively efficient way to prioritize those needs. Other school personnel could be contacted in a similar way. The counselors realized, however, that they really wanted information from those persons who would choose (or not choose) to be in the groups: the students. They also believed that a survey of all students would do more than help them plan the groups; the survey also could inform students of the counseling services available to them at Crest.

Thus, as a method of addressing both of their goals, the counselors decided to incorporate a needs assessment survey of all students into their orientation sessions. These sessions would be conducted in each homeroom during the first weeks of school. The counselors realized that this would be a large project, and that a random survey of students could provide reliable and valid information. Nevertheless, they wanted to give each student a chance to provide input about the small groups.

Ms. Betts and Ms. Healy reviewed their list of group topics with several aims in mind. First, they were concerned about the length of the list; they didn't want to overwhelm the students or take up too much time during the homeroom period. They carefully checked for duplicated and overlapping items to narrow the list. Second, they wanted to include at least one item for each student competency area (i.e., educational, career, personal, and social development; see Indicator 7.9). Finally, they also wanted to address unique needs of their student population, such as the high turnover rate. After much discussion, they decided on 10 group topics: study skills, making the transition from elementary to middle school, peer pressure, handling anger, self-esteem, parental divorce, girlfriend/boyfriend issues, making friends, preparing to go to high school, and career planning.

Creating the Needs Assessment Survey

As a check on their needs assessment list, Ms. Betts and Ms. Healy asked two groups to review the topics and to suggest any changes. First, they went to 10 teachers who had worked closely with them in the past. The teachers said that the list represented students' most common and important concerns. Then the counselors met with student council officers; this group suggested that "catchy titles" (rather than a mere listing of topics) would get their classmates' attention and interest. Working with these officers, the counselors reworded the items for the needs assessment questionnaire.

The counselors considered several questionnaire formats, including a Likert scale (ratings on a 5-point scale), yes/no responses, and rank ordering. To simplify the task of responding, yet maximize the amount of information they would get, they chose a two-step procedure: asking students to (a) circle "yes" or "no" to indicate interest in each group topic and then to (b) circle the topic of first priority. In this way, the counselors would get an indication of which group(s) to offer first and which to plan for during the rest of the school year. Their final questionnaire is reproduced in Figure 1.1.

Administration of the Questionnaire

Standardizing Administration of the Survey

Ms. Betts and Ms. Healy designed their classroom orientation sessions to enhance the likelihood of getting reliable and valid results. They wrote a script that they would use in each classroom, thus standardizing the administration of the questionnaire. After each counselor had used the script with one homeroom, they met and discussed whether any changes were needed. Because of their thorough preparation, none seemed necessary.

The counselors scheduled a 20-minute session with each homeroom. Using the prepared script, they first introduced the counselors and the counseling program, then described plans for the small groups, the ways that groups are helpful (e.g., to get to know more students, to share common concerns and generate solutions), and how these groups would be organized and conducted (e.g., sign-up sheets, meetings during rotating class periods). The counselors emphasized that they wanted to offer groups that the students preferred and so were seeking their input via a questionnaire.

Which Is *Your* Small Group?

School Counseling

Crest Middle School

Ms. Betts and Ms. Healy will meet with small groups of students this year to discuss a variety of topics. The group topics listed below will be explained during homeroom. Please wait for directions to begin.

YES	NO	1.	Getting It All Done (or, Homework in Middle School Sure Is Different From Elementary School)
YES	NO	2.	Will I Fit in at Crest Middle School?
YES	NO	3.	How to Say "No" to Drugs and Still Have Friends
YES	NO	4.	When I'm Angry I Just Want To . . .
YES	NO	5.	I'd Like Myself Better If . . .
YES	NO	6.	When Parents Get a Divorce
YES	NO	7.	Are We Boyfriend/Girlfriend? (or, John Told Paul to Tell Betty to Tell Ellen That He Thinks He Likes Her)
YES	NO	8.	Why Make New Friends When I'll Move Away and Miss Them?
YES	NO	9.	What's High School All About?
YES	NO	10.	How Am I Supposed to Know What I Want to Be When I Grow Up?

Use the space below to write any comments or suggestions for your school counselors.

Figure 1.1. Needs Assessment Questionnaire

Protecting Confidentiality

After distributing the questionnaire, the counselors explained that the students should not put their names or initials on the paper (to ensure confidentiality) and that the students did not have to participate if they chose not to for any reason (to ensure informed consent). Those who chose not to participate did not have to say this; they could just turn in their blank papers along with the others at the end of the presentation.

Following their script carefully, the counselors gave a brief description for each item and then asked the students to circle "yes" or "no" to indicate whether they would be interested in that group. For example, the script for Item 4 ("When I'm Angry I Just Want To . . .") read as follows:

> We all feel angry at times, and it's certainly OK to feel angry. But we don't always know what to do when we feel angry. We know it's not OK to fight or yell at someone, whether we're at school or at home. But it's really hard to hold that anger inside and walk around mad all day. If you aren't sure what to do when you're angry and would like to be in a group to discuss anger, circle "yes"

for item number 4. If you aren't interested in that group, circle "no" for item number 4.

After reading through all of the items, the counselors asked, "Where do we start? There's probably one group you are more interested in than the others on the list. Please go back and circle the group you would like us to offer first."

Finally, the counselors provided a few minutes for the students to write any comments they had at the bottom of the questionnaire.

Results of the Survey of Students

Organizing the Information

Ms. Betts and Ms. Healy kept each homeroom's questionnaires in a separate envelope, labeled only by grade level. They first planned to tally the results for two randomly selected homerooms for each grade. This procedure seemed acceptable, because students were assigned to homerooms alphabetically (rather than by ability level or other factors). But then the counselors realized that some homerooms might have a large representation of a particular ethnic group, which would bias the sample. At that point, Ms. Betts and Ms. Healy decided to tabulate the results of all students. They asked members of the school's parent association to help them tally the results. The counselors' instructions to the team of parent volunteers for each grade level of surveys included the following:

1. Pull out blank or incomplete questionnaires.
2. Count the number of "yes" responses to each item.
3. Count the number of times each item is circled as the first choice.
4. Type a verbatim copy of the comments and suggestions students write at the bottom of the survey questionnaire.

Three weeks later, the parent team delivered the results displayed in Table 1.1.

Interpretation of the Results

Students' self-reported needs were fairly obvious from the results, as were similarities and differences across the three grades. Sixth graders seemed quite concerned about succeeding academically and socially during their first year in middle school. A large number of them, however, also requested help in dealing with divorce. The latter result illustrated the different information gained from the two types of responses: Item 6 received the third-highest number of "yes" responses, but the most first-choice responses. Apparently, the students who were dealing with divorce were in some distress.

TABLE 1.1 Results of the Student Survey as Compiled by the Parent Team

Group Topic	Total "Yes" Responses	Number of First-Choice Responses
Grade 6		
1. Homework	83	25
2. Fitting in	99	45
3. "No" to drugs	30	11
4. Handling anger	16	0
5. Self-esteem	37	8
6. Parental divorce	70	61
7. Boyfriend/girlfriend	44	6
8. Moving away	22	0
9. High school	13	0
10. Career planning	8	0
Total Responses	422	156
Grade 7		
1. Homework	12	0
2. Fitting in	26	0
3. "No" to drugs	97	42
4. Handling anger	99	8
5. Self-esteem	105	38
6. Parental divorce	14	6
7. Boyfriend/girlfriend	92	34
8. Moving away	73	3
9. High school	58	2
10. Career planning	19	0
Total Responses	595	133
Grade 8		
1. Homework	0	0
2. Fitting in	12	0
3. "No" to drugs	53	12
4. Handling anger	22	2
5. Self-esteem	48	3
6. Parental divorce	16	0
7. Boyfriend/girlfriend	62	10
8. Moving away	19	2
9. High school	83	61
10. Career planning	31	10
Total Responses	356	100

Comparing Responses by Grade Level

Seventh graders gave the most "yes" responses overall, indicating a wide variety of concerns. In particular, these students seemed to be interested in self-esteem issues (Item 5), but they also indicated concerns with peer pressure (Item 3) and male-female relationships (Item 7). Other relationship issues, such as expressing anger (Item 4) and the pressures of frequent moves on establishing friendships (Item 8) also received a large number of "yes" responses.

Eighth graders were more focused on the future, already concerned about the transition to high school (Item 9) and wondering about career choices (Item 10). Male-female relationships (Item 7) and peer pressure (Item 3) also figured prominently in some eighth graders' minds.

Finally, a typed summary of comments and suggestions indicated that students appreciated counselors' explanations of the counseling program and, in general, were eager to take advantage of the various counseling services. A number wrote questions, however, concerning small group composition and confidentiality.

Applying the Results and Interpretation

Planning Small Groups Based on the Results

Students' responses to the needs assessment questionnaire provided several directions for planning small groups. Ms. Betts and Ms. Healy made several decisions based on the results. First, they decided to give priority and primary emphasis to the seventh graders, who seemed to have the greatest number of concerns (see Indicator 6.8). Despite the counselors' interest in using small groups, they decided to address self-esteem, peer pressure, and anger issues through classroom guidance; it appeared these were quite prevalent needs. They also offered to consult with the seventh-grade teachers about including these issues in their regular course activities. They planned to identify students for follow-up small groups through these classroom interventions.

Sixth graders were most concerned about adjusting to middle school. Ms. Betts and Ms. Healy had been leading guidance units related to this topic for several years, and the results supported continuation of their efforts. One change was indicated, however: At least one session would be devoted to study skills. There also was a strong need for a series of small groups focusing on dealing with divorce.

In the past, Ms. Betts and Ms. Healy had met with eighth graders during spring registration for their high school. The results of the needs assessment, however, indicated the students already were quite concerned about making the transition to high school. Thus the counselors made plans for earlier interventions, including visits by previous Crest students to each eighth-grade homeroom.

Although some students' concerns were unique to a particular grade level, some general needs were indicated. Ms. Betts and Ms. Healy began to consider the possibility of cross-grade small groups for some topics, such as peer pressure (Item 3) and making and leaving friends (Item 8).

Summary of Evaluation Principles

This example illustrates several important principles that should be kept in mind when conducting any needs assessment. These principles include the following:

1. Students (and parents, teachers, etc.) have a right not to respond. They should be provided this right with no penalty, in a way that does not require them to broadcast their decision.
2. Students (and parents, teachers, etc.) are more likely to give honest answers if their responses are confidential. If possible, anonymous responses are preferred.
3. Sometimes it is too cumbersome (or expensive) to give a needs assessment to an entire student population. If Crest's student population had been much larger than 450, a random survey would have been a better choice in terms of time and effort. (See Chapter 3 in the general guide for an explanation of sampling procedures.)
4. Needs assessments should be based on particular program goals. In this case, the counselors devised a strategy to meet two program goals: meeting/informing students and determining which small groups to offer. The items also were written to reflect specific student competency areas (i.e., educational, career, personal, and social development). Program goals and competency areas provided a framework for designing a relevant needs assessment questionnaire.
5. Needs assessment procedures should reflect the specific concerns of a particular evaluation. Here it is relevant to remember one difference between evaluation and research: Our motive in needs assessments is not to generalize to other populations but to serve a particular student body.
6. Needs assessments should be tied directly to program planning and program evaluation. In this case, for example, the counselors chose specific interventions based on the results. They also could use the same questionnaire as an evaluation instrument. One global measure of their effectiveness would be a decrease in the number of "yes" responses to the group topics they targeted during the school year.
7. A standardized administration procedure is highly desirable. In this case, the counselors wrote a script that both of them could follow to be sure that students understood the items and that the same explanations were given in each administration.
8. Items should be written in language that will heighten respondents' interest and elicit completion of a questionnaire.
9. Pilot testing of an instrument is strongly recommended. In this example, the counselors consulted with teachers and student council officers; the latter offered valuable feedback. Such procedures help to improve an instrument in addition to building goodwill.

Alternative Strategies

Other Sources of Information

The counselors in this example surveyed the population of interest: the students who would receive the services. As Indicator 8.5 suggests, they also might have given the questionnaire to parents, teachers, and other school personnel. Multiple sources often provide instructive information. In this case, for example, the counselors could have compared students' self-reported needs and parents' (or teachers') perceptions of those needs.

Other Methods of Collecting Information

In addition, other data collection methods could have been used, such as structured interviews or focus groups. These two approaches probably would have yielded more detailed information about students' concerns (e.g., eighth graders' specific concerns about high school) but would have taken much more time, involved fewer students, and required outside interviewers. In addition, commercial instruments that assess students' concerns are available (e.g., the Mooney Problem Checklist). Using these standardized instruments would have allowed counselors to compare students' responses to norm groups but would have been more costly. In addition, items of particular relevance to this school might not have been represented in the standardized checklist. (See Chapter 3 in the general guide for explanations on how to plan various types of evaluation methods and create various types of instruments.)

Cautions Regarding Misinterpretation

Limitations of the Survey

The value of an assessment instrument is determined, in part, by the validity of its items. A 10-item questionnaire is, of necessity, incomplete. In this case, for example, there were no questions regarding a student's relationship with his or her parents or siblings. The use of anonymous questionnaires meant the counselors could not identify whether subgroups of students (e.g., gifted students, high-risk students, athletes) had special needs. Readers might identify other concerns they think are central to middle school students and/or to their particular student body. Thus the results gleaned from this questionnaire provide accurate reflections of students in one particular school during one time period in response to 10 specific items. Generalization to other student needs for counseling or guidance services is unwarranted.

2 Vignette Two

Evaluating Individual Counseling Services

Winton County, North Carolina, spreads across the foothills of the Blue Ridge Mountains. It is a largely rural county supported by family-run farms and moderately sized industrial textile mills. Broadview Elementary School draws its K-5 students from three of Winton County's midsized towns—one made up largely of family-owned and operated farms of various sizes and fortune, one largely consisting of textile mills, and one favoring goods and services. Hispanic students make up roughly 2% of the total number of students enrolled at Broadview; black students make up 24%, and the remaining 73% are non-Hispanic whites.

This is Sue Melton's first year as a full-time counselor at Broadview Elementary School. Prior to this year, Ms. Melton, like other elementary counselors in Winton County, filled two half-time counselor positions, one at Broadview and one at another elementary school in the county. Although Ms. Melton has always enjoyed good working relationships with the school personnel at Broadview and knows many of the students and parents, working half-time limits her capacity to implement certain program components. Now that she is working there full-time, Ms. Melton intends to develop a comprehensive school counseling program at Broadview.

Individual Counseling Services 21

Focusing the Evaluation

From the beginning, Ms. Melton realizes that ongoing evaluation will be essential to developing and sustaining a quality comprehensive program. She knows she can rely on the principal, teachers, staff, and parents at Broadview to support her ongoing program evaluation efforts. The principal was instrumental in garnering a full-time counselor position for Broadview, and everyone there wants to see a comprehensive school counseling program developed. Ongoing evaluation will give them information about the effectiveness of various aspects of that program.

Ongoing (or formative) evaluation means routinely collecting information (or data) on program activities throughout the year. Evaluating program activities throughout the year will enable Ms. Melton to do two things. First, she can evaluate the effectiveness of a particular type of intervention. Collecting data on a specific intervention, such as individual or group counseling, can reveal the strengths and weaknesses of that intervention with a particular student or group of students. Second, Ms. Melton can summarize the data she routinely collects on each type of intervention. This will enable her to identify areas in which a majority of the students either have or have not achieved the goals of a particular intervention. Summary data from each type of intervention can be used with other information for an end-of-year, or summative, evaluation to determine the overall effectiveness of the program. (See Chapter 2 in the general guide for an expanded discussion of formative and summative evaluations.)

Ms. Melton in the past has focused on implementing and evaluating group counseling and classroom guidance because of time constraints. Now that she is at Broadview full-time, she will expand individual counseling and wants to focus evaluation on this program component. Ms. Melton reviews the standards and indicators for evaluating school counseling programs (see Resource A) to guide her evaluation planning. Because of her interest in assessing a particular program component, Ms. Melton selects Indicator 9.1 ("Evaluation results indicate a majority of students achieve program goals and/or meet specified competencies").

Strategy for Collecting Information

One example of Ms. Melton's ongoing efforts to evaluate individual counseling using Indicator 9.1 involves the use of a behavior checklist. Tommy is a second grader who was referred to Ms. Melton by his teacher, Ms. Hartley, because of disruptive behavior during instruction. Ms. Melton chose a behavioral approach to individual counseling with Tommy, because his problems centered around behavior that could be defined and monitored easily. Before beginning her sessions with Tommy, she considered ways in which she would evaluate the effectiveness of this type of individual counseling intervention with him.

Matching the Evaluation Method to the Counseling Intervention

She thought about using classroom observations, which could provide information about Tommy's interactions with his peers and with Ms. Hartley during classroom instruction. An observer could monitor specific behavior and could provide an overall impression of what was taking place when Tommy behaved or misbehaved.

Ms. Melton wondered who she would get to do the classroom observations. She preferred someone who had no investment in the results of the observations; that is, someone who had nothing to gain or lose by what he or she recorded. There was no other counselor at Broadview she could ask to observe Tommy, and she did not want to ask another teacher to spend coveted "free" time making observations. A trained volunteer parent also was a possibility, but locating and training such a parent would require more time than Ms. Melton had available to her. Therefore, Ms. Melton looked for another alternative to evaluate the impact of individual counseling on Tommy's classroom behavior.

Several texts on school counseling programs suggested the use of behavior checklists in program evaluation. A behavior checklist is relatively simple to complete, requiring only that a teacher check "yes" for each behavior on the checklist observed and "no" for each behavior on the checklist not observed. Using this method, Ms. Melton could work with Ms. Hartley to specify appropriate classroom behaviors for second graders and to target the behaviors Tommy needed to improve. Ms. Melton could then construct a checklist consisting of the appropriate classroom behaviors and use the checklist to help Tommy set realistic goals for improving the targeted behaviors. Once the goals for improvement were agreed upon, Ms. Melton could proceed with individual counseling with Tommy. Checklists could be used on a weekly basis to monitor Tommy's progress.

Creating a Behavior Checklist

Ms. Melton constructed a behavior checklist consisting of appropriate classroom behaviors for second graders, which would allow her to use the checklist with other second-grade students. She limited the number of behaviors to 10 because she did not want to burden the teacher with a lengthy list. She was careful to include a couple of behaviors Tommy had already mastered, because she wanted Tommy to work from his strengths rather than his weaknesses. All behaviors were stated as expectations and not requirements that undesirable behaviors must cease. For example, Tommy was having a hard time not talking during instruction. Ms. Melton phrased the behavior as she would like it to be ("speaks at appropriate times") rather than what she would like Tommy to stop doing ("stops talking out of turn"). The final behavior checklist is shown in Figure 2.1. When she had completed the checklist, Ms. Melton helped Ms. Hartley set realistic parameters, or boundaries, for approving each behavior on the checklist. For example, how consistently would Tommy have to talk at appropriate times in order for Ms. Hartley to check "yes" for this behavior?

Ms. Hartley completed the first checklist prior to the onset of individual counseling. After she had completed the first checklist, Ms. Melton asked her to prioritize the target behaviors (those behaviors checked "no") in terms of which behaviors she would like to see improved first, second, third, and so on. Ms. Melton and Ms. Hartley also talked about how to handle improvements as well as possible lags and/or setbacks in target behaviors.

Collecting Baseline Information

The first checklist served as a *baseline* for Tommy's classroom behavior, a comparison checklist for subsequent weeks. The baseline data informed Ms. Hartley, Tommy, and Ms. Melton which behaviors needed improvement before individual counseling began; it provided a starting point from which Ms. Melton could evaluate Tommy's progress throughout the course of counseling.

Administration of the Checklist

Ms. Melton left a behavior checklist in Ms. Hartley's box each Friday morning. At the end of the day, Ms. Hartley reflected on Tommy's behavior throughout the week. She checked "yes" beside each behavior if Tommy had consistently adhered to it and "no" if he had not. At the bottom of the behavior checklist, Ms. Hartley wrote additional comments, such as "Tommy is getting better about remaining seated, but he is still not doing so consistently."

Results of the Behavior Checklist

Ms. Melton and Ms. Hartley agreed to evaluate Tommy's behavior, using the same checklist, at the end of each week until Tommy had achieved the goals for improving classroom behavior, or until an alternative strategy was in place. Ms. Melton recorded the results of Ms. Hartley's baseline behavior checklist in a table (see Table 2.1), placing an N beside the behavior if Ms. Hartley had checked "no" and a Y beside the behavior if Ms. Hartley had checked "yes." She did this each week, using each completed checklist.

Broadview Elementary School
Behavior Checklist (Second Grade)

Directions: Please check "yes" or "no" under the appropriate column for each behavior based on *(student's name)*'s performance in your classroom for the week *(beginning and ending dates)*. Please be sure to judge each of the 10 behaviors based on *(student's name)*'s performance in your class.

Yes	No	
___	___	Is seated properly in his/her chair
___	___	Remains seated at appropriate times
___	___	Is prepared (has pencil, paper, and book) for instruction
___	___	Speaks at appropriate times
___	___	Obtains permission before leaving his/her seat during instruction
___	___	Treats property of others with care
___	___	Shares classroom materials when asked
___	___	Uses appropriate language when addressing the teacher and others
___	___	Gets along with his/her peers
___	___	Completes seatwork on time

Please add any additional comments in the space below.

Figure 2.1. Behavior Checklist

Organizing the Information

The goals of the individual counseling intervention were achieved in 6 weeks. To summarize the results, Ms. Melton totaled the number of N's she had recorded for the baseline and during each of the subsequent weeks for each behavior on the checklist. The results are shown in Table 2.1.

Determining Weekly Progress

At baseline, Ms. Hartley checked "no" for 6 of the 10 behaviors on the checklist: "is seated properly," "remains seated," "is prepared for instruction," "speaks at appropriate times," "obtains permission before leaving his seat during instruction," and "completes seatwork on time." She checked "yes" for 4 out of the 10 behaviors on the checklist: "treats property of others with care," "shares classroom materials when asked," "uses appropriate language" (when addressing the teacher and others), and "gets along with peers."

Identical results were obtained at the end of the first week of individual counseling with Tommy. After 2 weeks of individual counseling, Ms. Hartley checked "yes" to two of the target behaviors: "is seated properly" and "remains seated." According to Ms. Hartley,

TABLE 2.1 Results of the Behavior Checklist

Behavior	Baseline	Week of Counseling					
		1	2	3	4	5	6
Is seated properly	N	N	Y	Y	Y	Y	Y
Remains seated	N	N	Y	Y	Y	Y	Y
Is prepared	N	N	N	Y	Y	Y	Y
Speaks at appropriate times	N	N	N	N	Y	Y	Y
Obtains permission before leaving his seat during instruction	N	N	N	N	N	N	Y
Treats property of others with care	Y	Y	Y	Y	Y	Y	Y
Shares classroom materials when asked	Y	Y	Y	Y	Y	Y	Y
Uses appropriate language	Y	Y	Y	Y	Y	Y	Y
Gets along with peers	Y	Y	Y	Y	Y	Y	Y
Completes seatwork on time	N	N	N	N	N	N	Y
Total Number of Ns	6	6	4	3	2	2	0

Tommy now was performing 6 out of the 10 behaviors on the checklist. After 3 weeks of individual counseling with Ms. Melton, Ms. Hartley checked "yes" to the target behavior "is prepared for instruction," leaving three behaviors that still needed improvement. At the end of the fourth week of individual counseling, Ms. Hartley checked "yes" to "speaks at appropriate times." After 6 weeks of individual counseling, Ms. Hartley indicated that Tommy was consistently performing all 10 of the behaviors on the behavior checklist.

Interpretation of the Results

Examining the Effectiveness of the Checklist

The checklist was focused, by design, on individual behaviors that could be identified easily by the teacher in the classroom. It is evident from Table 2.1 above that Ms. Hartley saw a substantial improvement in Tommy's classroom behavior. In addition, once Tommy had received a "yes" on a behavior, he did not revert to "no" for the duration of his individual counseling with Ms. Melton. After 6 weeks of individual counseling, Tommy had received a "yes" for all ten behaviors on the checklist. Will Tommy maintain his improved classroom behaviors when he no longer sees Ms. Melton for individual counseling. Follow-up administrations of the behavior checklist would provide this information.

Several of the behaviors on the behavior checklist seem closely related; that is, a change regarding one behavior would likely affect a related behavior. For example, establishing the behavior "is seated properly" would likely affect the behavior "remains seated," given that being seated properly may be part of remaining seated or vice versa. This may explain why these two behaviors were achieved during the same week.

The behavior "obtains permission before leaving his seat during instruction" seems to coincide with "is seated properly" and "remains seated"; however, the former was not achieved until the sixth week of counseling. Tommy was remaining seated by the second week. Perhaps he stopped *asking* to leave his seat as well. Ms. Hartley could not check "yes" to Tommy obtaining permission to leave his seat if she had not observed him doing so. This identifies a weakness of the yes/no format for a behavior checklist. In this case, "no" may have indicated inappropriate behavior or no chance to observe. Ms. Melton may want to omit or revise this item, because it is a classroom behavior that may or may not occur.

It is possible that sitting properly and remaining seated enabled Tommy to focus on preparing his materials, which in turn led to his speaking at appropriate times. Once Tommy had these behaviors under control, it would be easier for him to complete homework assignments. Whatever the reason, it is apparent from the above results that Tommy began to improve his classroom behavior after individual counseling commenced and continued to improve his classroom behavior throughout the course of the intervention.

Applying the Results and Interpretation

Using Results to Plan Individual Counseling Sessions

In this case, Ms. Melton used the behavior checklist at the end of each week until Tommy had achieved the behavioral goals of the individual counseling intervention. Obtaining Ms. Hartley's feedback on the results of the behavior checklist completed after 1 week of individual counseling helped Ms. Melton to determine fairly early whether or not individual counseling was having an impact on Tommy's behavior. Tommy's behavior either improved or maintained each week he received individual counseling; his behavior did not veer from this positive trend. The results indicate that Ms. Melton was successful (i.e., her individual counseling intervention appeared to be appropriate with this student).

Throughout the coming year, Ms. Melton will use the behavior checklist with other students in individual counseling and will record the results for each student in a summary table. She also will collect information from other methods she uses to evaluate individual counseling and record the results in a summary table designed for each method. Together, the results from various methods for evaluating individual counseling will be used in an end-of-year, or summative, evaluation of Broadview's school counseling program. At that time, the overall results of individual counseling will be tallied, and

Individual Counseling Services 27

the weaknesses and strengths of this program component will be revealed.

Summary of Evaluation Principles

This example illustrated several important principles that should be kept in mind in all evaluations of school programs. As in other examples in this guide, we provide a list of these principles:

1. When choosing a method of data collection, try to select an alternative that minimizes the burden on those who will be asked to provide information. In this case, a brief checklist focused on specific behaviors and required little time for the teacher to complete it.
2. Ask questions your information providers are able to answer, and avoid questions that require speculation. Remember that behaviors can be observed, but judgments concerning attitudes are speculative. In this case, Ms. Hartley was asked to check the behaviors she had observed Tommy performing during classroom instruction. She was not asked to rate Tommy's attitude toward school, nor the *quality* of his behavior or seatwork.
3. Make sure that behaviors are defined clearly and understood by all persons involved in the evaluation of the behaviors. In this example, Ms. Melton met with the teacher to define and clarify classroom behaviors and reviewed these definitions with Tommy, the student.
4. Checklist behaviors should be written as goals, not failures. In this example, Ms. Melton listed the behaviors she and Ms. Hartley wanted Tommy to achieve, rather than those Ms. Hartley wanted to extinguish. (See Chapter 3 in the general guide for a further discussion of behavior checklists.)

Alternative Strategies

Other Sources of Information

In addition to a checklist, Ms. Melton could have used unobtrusive measures of Tommy's behavior. For example, she could have tallied the number of discipline referrals for Tommy and compared the number of referrals before counseling to the number of referrals at the end of counseling. (See Chapter 3 in the general guide for an explanation of unobtrusive measures.)

Direct Versus Indirect Observations

As previously discussed, Tommy could have been observed directly by someone other than Ms. Melton or Ms. Hartley. Direct observation might provide more objective information; for example, Ms. Hartley would not have to remember how consistently Tommy's behavior had been over the past week. An outside observer also would reduce the chance that the results were influenced by any vested interest on the part of the observer. Direct observation, however, requires available observers, time for training, and the development of a system for collecting the observation information. Ms. Melton did not have someone readily available. She also wanted to assist Ms. Hartley in reducing Tommy's disruptive behaviors as soon as possible.

Cautions Regarding Misinterpretation

Other Possible Explanations for the Results

It is clear that something or a series of some things affected Tommy's behavior during the 6 weeks in which he was receiving individual counseling from Ms. Melton. It would be a mistake, however, to ignore factors other than individual counseling that may have influenced Tommy's behavior. The behavior checklist identifies behaviors, but it does not indicate what factors influenced any changes. It may be that Tommy's father, who had been separated from the family since the beginning of the year, returned during the time Tommy was receiving individual counseling from Ms. Melton. The results may be attributable in part to the fact that Ms. Hartley began a new unit on dinosaurs that Tommy relished. Tommy's mother, aware that Tommy was having problems at school, may have offered him $10 if he was able to do all the things the teacher said he should. Ms. Hartley may have begun to interact differently with Tommy, thus affecting his classroom behaviors, or she may have perceived his behavior differently once he began individual counseling with Ms. Melton.

A second caveat regarding the results of Ms. Melton's evaluation of her individual counseling program activity is that we do not know whether the results of the behavior checklist will be lasting. The fact that Tommy was receiving regular attention from the school counselor may have contributed greatly to the change in his behavior in the classroom. Once individual counseling is discontinued, Tommy may revert back to his old behaviors. Would this mean that whatever Ms. Melton was doing was working, but that she did not do it long enough? Or would it mean that the real problem was not addressed in counseling, only masked by Tommy's apparent need for attention? It may be that Tommy will need intermittent (i.e., occasional) sessions with Ms. Melton, either individually or in a small group, in order to maintain his positive behaviors. In any case, it would be wise for Ms. Melton to follow up with Ms. Hartley regarding Tommy, either informally or through another checklist.

Replicating the Evaluation Procedure

Sue Melton intends to strengthen the link between individual counseling and student outcomes by replicating the procedure she used to evaluate Tommy's improvement. Now that Ms. Melton has developed a behavior checklist, she can select students with concerns

Individual Counseling Services 29

similar to Tommy's, employ the same individual counseling techniques for the same length of time, and use the behavior checklist to evaluate pre-and postcounseling behavior. She can adapt this checklist for use with older or younger students as well. Successful replications would suggest that this particular individual counseling approach is effective with students who have classroom behavior problems.

Replications also may indicate that different interventions are needed for some types of students or other behavior problems. Ms. Melton can modify the behavior checklist to evaluate these interventions, or she can use another method of evaluation. By summarizing all evaluation data collected on individual counseling interventions and other counseling methods throughout the year, Ms. Melton can determine whether a majority of her students have achieved the goals of individual counseling, the criterion set forth in Indicator 9.1 (see page 31).

3

Vignette Three

Using Control Groups in Program Evaluation

Ventura Middle School enrolls 667 students in grades 6, 7, and 8. It draws students from all sections of Sautern, Maine, a coastal city of 50,000 that is supported by fishing and canning, tourism, and a moderately sized 4-year university. Students bused to Ventura come from neighborhoods representing all economic levels. About 40% of the school's pupils are black; the rest are white.

Ms. Taylor and Ms. Parrish, counselors at Ventura Middle School, planned their program at the beginning of the year, prioritizing program goals and objectives according to the results of recently conducted needs assessments. Because many of the concerns given high priority by students, teachers, and parents fell into the social competency area, the two counselors decided to give this area priority in their program.

The two counselors focused program activities in the area of social competency around small group counseling. By counseling students who share similar concerns in groups, Ms. Taylor and Ms. Parrish would be able to reach more students than could be seen individually. Also, unlike classroom guidance, small groups would create "practice" peer groups that would allow students with similar concerns to explore, try out, and support new or augmented skills under the auspices of a counselor. Ms. Taylor and Ms. Parrish decided that each would run a series of groups on various topics relating to social competency throughout the school year. Groups would be problem oriented and/or developmentally based.

Focusing the Evaluation

Ms. Taylor and Ms. Parrish were proud of their systematic approach to planning and implementing their school counseling program and wanted to evaluate their program's effectiveness for two reasons. First, they wanted to know which aspects of their program to maintain or enhance and which to improve or eliminate. Second, they wanted to be able to communicate their program's effectiveness to students, teachers, administrators, and the community.

Ms. Taylor and Ms. Parrish planned to implement a program that expanded and focused small group counseling activities in the area of social competency. This represented a new dimension to their program, one the two counselors wanted to evaluate. They referred to the list of standards and indicators for evaluating school counseling programs (see Resource A) and selected an indicator that would enable them to determine whether most of their students had benefited from their systematic efforts.

Indicator 9.1. Evaluation results indicate a majority of students achieve program goals and/or meet specified competencies.

Strategy for Collecting Information

Defining the Goals of the Small Group

Proceeding with the program goals, Ms. Taylor and Ms. Parrish planned their small groups. Ms. Taylor named one of her first groups "Peering Up." This group consisted of seventh-grade students who were having difficulty making and/or keeping friends, a concern that was identified frequently by seventh-grade students and teachers at Ventura. It was clear from Indicator 9.1 that Ms. Taylor needed to collect information that would reveal whether or not most of the students in her group achieved the goals of the intervention. The broad goal for Peering Up was social competency; because Ms. Taylor wanted to keep the evaluation of her interventions as specific as possible, she narrowed the definition of social competency in this case to the appropriate use of communication skills.

Ms. Taylor outlined her objectives by listing the specific communication skills she planned to target through her group intervention: making eye contact; sitting square to the speaker; employing appropriate verbal and nonverbal listening skills; asking appropriate questions; giving and receiving compliments; and not picking on others. Ms. Taylor planned to help students in the group evaluate the effectiveness of their verbal and nonverbal messages and to facilitate group exploration of effective communication skills. Once students in the group had been given the opportunity to explore, students would practice effective communication skills by participating in role-playing situations and by completing homework assignments.

Using a Control Group

Ms. Taylor wanted to limit the size of her group to 7 students, but 14 students signed up. She wanted to give all 14 students an opportunity to participate, so she decided to run a second Peering Up group later. She mentioned this idea to Ms. Parrish, who suggested that Ms. Taylor use the students who would not participate in the group until later as a control group. Ms. Parrish explained that a control group would enable Ms. Taylor to compare the communication skills of students in group counseling with students not in group counseling and allow Ms. Taylor to "control for" extraneous influences, like individual differences, on the evaluation results. If the students in the counseling group improved in their communication skills and the students in the control group did not, Ms. Taylor could be more certain that students improved their communication skills because of their participation in group counseling and not because of some outside influence.

Ms. Parrish described how a control group would work. The control group and counseling group would consist of the same number of students who were having similar difficulties. Because Ms. Taylor had 14 students who were having trouble making and keeping friends, 7 of these students would participate in group counseling first and 7 would participate in group counseling later. Based on this approach, Ms. Taylor would collect information on both groups while the first series of group meetings was being conducted. Information would be collected before counseling began and again when counseling ended. Ms. Taylor expected to find that a majority of the students in the counseling group would have achieved the goals of Peering Up. In contrast, she expected a majority of the students in the control group would not have achieved these goals.

Making Random Assignments of Students to the Groups

Having decided to use a control group, Ms. Taylor was ready to assign each of the 14 students to one of the two groups. She wanted to make certain that students were not assigned to either group for any reason other than chance, because she did not want a *selection effect* to occur. If, for example, students were selected for the counseling group based on Ms. Taylor's belief that their need for services was more acute than that of other students, Ms. Taylor only would have information on the impact of her group on students with the *worst* communication skills and not on students with a relatively normal range of communication skills. It therefore would be difficult for her to surmise that her group would benefit a variety of students in the future.

To accomplish a random assignment of students to the groups, Ms. Taylor wrote each student's name on a separate piece of paper and placed the 14 pieces of paper in a bag. After shaking the bag well, she drew the pieces of paper out of the bag one at a time. She tossed a coin to determine whether the student drawn would be in the counseling group or in the control group. If the coin landed heads up, the student was assigned to the counseling group. If the coin landed tails up, the student was assigned to the control group. She repeated this procedure until seven students had been assigned to the counseling group. The others were assigned to the control group.

Choosing the Method of Data Collection

Finally, Ms. Taylor had to decide what data to collect and how it would be collected. The same information needed to be collected on both groups of students. She considered constructing a written test to determine whether or not students in either group had achieved the goals of the Peering Up group; however, testing would only measure the students' knowledge and not their actual behavior. The same would be true of a written questionnaire.

She also considered using a behavior checklist, but a checklist would require a teacher to reflect upon students' interaction in a social setting—a setting in which the teacher might not have an opportunity to observe systematically. She could have teachers rate students, but she was afraid that it would be difficult for teachers to separate either past behavior from new behavior or instructional behavior from social behavior, given that improvement might be subtle.

Observations are relatively unobtrusive; that is, information is obtained without the subject of the observation knowing about it. Observations also can take into account the *context* in which a behavior occurs. For example, an observer can note the noise level of a classroom, describe the activity taking place, and record the number and/or duration of verbal and nonverbal interactions between two or more people. Ms. Taylor wanted this type of information. Because Ms. Taylor wanted to ensure that all students had the same opportunity to interact in a social (rather than classroom) situation, she decided to conduct observations during the students' lunch period.

The Observation Instrument

Ms. Taylor needed to construct an observation instrument and then train observers to use the instrument. First, Ms. Taylor used the list of objectives for her group to describe what an observer would see if the student being observed was using the target communication skills appropriately. She was careful to avoid any inferences of value or meaning concerning a particular behavior when she worded an observation item. Based on the list of objectives, the observer would see the student respond to others, verbally or nonverbally, and look at others when interacting with them. The student would square his or her body toward the speaker, the shoulders appearing relaxed and open. The student would smile at others, initiate conversation by asking questions, and compliment others. The student would refrain from picking on others.

Creating an Observation Checklist

Ms. Taylor also described behaviors she expected an observer *not* to see if the student was applying the social skills taught in her group. The student would not look at peers or teachers, instead looking at his or her plate when speaking or listening. The student would slump, the shoulders apparently drawing inward, and the arms held rigidly close to the body. He or she would not face the speaker with a squared body. The student would probably sit alone through most of lunch or sit with other students without interacting. The student would not nod his or her head, smile, or appear actively involved during another's attempt to interact. The student would not question or compliment other students.

Wording every item on an instrument in the same way (either all positively or all negatively) can lead to a *response set,* that is, a tendency of the rater to agree with the general slant of the instrument. Thus, items 7 and 8 were written to measure change in the use of inappropriate, rather than appropriate, communication skills ("target student did not respond when approached by others" and "target student picked on others"). The final checklist that Ms. Taylor used is shown in Figure 3.1.

Training the Observers

Ms. Parrish, the other school counselor, and Mr. Lehman, the school nurse, agreed to do the observations. First, Ms. Taylor reviewed the instrument with her two observers, defining behaviors and clarifying items. For example, what constituted a compliment? What constituted a nonverbal response? What would be considered "picking on" as opposed to playful teasing?

Next, Ms. Taylor described the procedure for conducting the observation. The observers were to seat themselves as close to the target student as possible without disrupting what was taking place at the table. Ms. Taylor suggested that the observers make a lunch schedule that would allow them to arrive at the lunch room before their target students and settle themselves within observation range. Ms. Taylor warned the observers against talking to others during the observation. She encouraged them to be natural and relaxed, but to

Ventura Middle School
Observation Instrument

Directions: After the target student is seated with his/her lunch, please keep a tally of the number of times you observe the target student demonstrate the following behaviors during a 10-minute time period. You may use the blank spaces between items to keep your tally. After you have observed the student, circle the appropriate response and/or fill in the blanks.

Student Observed: _____ Time: From: _____ To: _____

Observer: _____ Date: _____

0 = This did not occur during the time of observation.

1 = This occurred once during the time of observation.

1+ ____ = This occurred more than once during the time of observation, and the approximate number of times it occurred was _____.

1. The target student smiled at others.	0	1	1+ ____
2. The target student spoke to others.	0	1	1+ ____
3. The target student looked at the person with whom he/she was speaking.	0	1	1+ ____
4. The target student squared his/her body to speaker.	0	1	1+ ____
5. The target student asked questions of others.	0	1	1+ ____
6. The target student complimented others.	0	1	1+ ____
7. The target student did not respond when approached by others.	0	1	1+ ____
8. The target student picked on others.	0	1	1+ ____

9. Based on your observation, please place a check beside the level of communication skill the target student demonstrated during this observation, using the scale provided below.

   _____ Unsatisfactory
   _____ Poor
   _____ So-so
   _____ Good
   _____ Outstanding

Please add any additional comments in the space provided below.

Figure 3.1. Observation Instrument

remain alert and focused. Each student would be observed for 10 minutes, once at the beginning and once at the end of group counseling.

Standardizing the Observations

After discussing the definitions and describing the procedure, Ms. Taylor trained the observers to record their observations. Each observer was instructed to keep a running tally of the number of times each of the seven communication skills was observed and to make notes regarding questions, comments, or difficulties encountered during the observation. At the end of the observation, each observer would total the number of times each of the seven communication skills was observed. The observer would circle "0" beside the item if the communication skill had not been observed, "1" beside the item if it had been observed only once, or "1+" beside the item if it had been observed more than once. In addition, if the communication had been observed more than once, the observer was instructed to record the total number of times it had been observed during the 10-minute observation. After the observers had entered the total number of times each item was observed, they were instructed to reflect on the overall observation and rate (based on their observation) the level of communication skill of the target student.

Ms. Parrish and Mr. Lehman first tested the instrument and their training. In order to establish whether or not Ms. Parrish and Mr. Lehman would see things similarly enough to consider their observations reliable or consistent, each observer rated the same students until they reached a consistent level. The two observers rated the first student the same on 50% of the items. They reported that a few of the items were still vague, requiring on-the-spot interpretation, and Ms. Taylor rewrote these items. A second student was observed by both Ms. Parrish and Mr. Lehman; this time, the observers agreed on 75% of the items. They discussed with Ms. Taylor the differences between the two observation records. The item "student's shoulders are relaxed and open" was acknowledged as being difficult to assess and was dropped from the instrument. Subsequent observation of a third student resulted in a 90% agreement between the two observers. The two observers now had achieved enough consistency in their respective observations to consider their ratings reliable.

Assigning Students for Observation

Making Random Assignments of Students to the Observers

Ms. Taylor wanted information on all 14 students that would show how they interacted before counseling began and how they interacted after 6 weeks; this would allow her to evaluate change in both the counseling and the control groups. Ms. Parrish and Mr. Lehman each would observe 7 students once during the week prior to the beginning of Ms. Taylor's group and once again during the week following the conclusion of the group sessions. To ensure that observers and students were paired by chance and not by design, the names of each of the 14 students were placed in a bag. The bag was shaken well, and Ms. Parrish and Mr. Lehman alternately drew names from the bag. The observers were not told whether their assigned students were in the counseling group or in the control group; neither were they informed as to the specific goals of the group. Keeping the observers blind to the specifics of the groups reduced the amount of information that could influence their observations. Ms. Parrish and Mr. Lehman scheduled two observations each day, according to their convenience, during the week prior to the first small group session. They followed a similar schedule the week following the last small group session.

Results of the Observation Instrument

Ms. Taylor began summarizing the results by pairing each student's pre- and postcounseling observation data. She then sorted the paired observation data according to whether the student was in the counseling group and the control group.

Comparing Pretest Scores to Posttest Scores

Next, she summarized the results by totaling the number of observations recorded beside each item for each student. She did this for the observations that were made before and after the small group meetings and recorded the totals beside the item in a summary table. Because she wanted to compare how much change had occurred during the 6 weeks of counseling, Ms. Taylor calculated a difference score by subtracting the precounseling scores from the postcounseling scores. Ms. Taylor indicated gains by using a "+" in front of the difference score. She indicated losses by using a "–" in front of the difference score. For example, if students had spoken more frequently with others during the postcounseling observation, the difference was considered a gain. If, however, the students had spoken less often with others during the postcounseling observation, the difference was considered a loss. Because items 7 and 8 were written to measure change in the use of inappropriate (rather than appropriate) communication skills, a *decrease* in the number of times each of these items was observed between pre- and postcounseling represented improvement. Ms. Taylor converted decreases between pre- and postcounseling on items 7 and 8 to "+" ratings for easier comparison. The results are shown in Table 3.1.

Determining the Average Change

Once Ms. Taylor had obtained the difference scores between the pre- and postcounseling observations for the counseling and control groups, she totaled the difference scores for each group. She added the pluses in the difference column for the counseling group (there were no minuses) and obtained a total of 57. To obtain the average, or mean, gain for this group, Ms. Taylor divided 57 by 8, the total number of items. The average overall improvement for the counseling group was 7.125, which she rounded to 7. Next, she calculated the

TABLE 3.1 Total Number of Times Students Were Observed Demonstrating Communication Skills, by Group, Pre- and Post-Counseling.

	Counseling Group (N = 7)			Control Group (N = 7)		
	Pre-	Post-	Difference	Pre-	Post-	Difference
1. Smiled at others	3	7	+4	2	4	+2
2. Spoke to others	6	18	+12	4	6	+2
3. Looked at person when interacting	0	15	+15	2	1	-1
4. Squared body to speaker	1	10	+9	0	0	—
5. Asked questions	0	5	+5	0	1	+1
6. Complimented others	0	6	+6	0	1	+1
7. Did not respond	5	1	+4*	4	4	—
8. Picked on others	4	2	+2*	6	5	+1*
Average difference		57 ÷ 8 = 7.125			6 ÷ 8 = 0.75	
9. Rating						
Unsatisfactory	2	—		3	3	
Poor	4	—		4	4	
So-so	1	1		—	—	
Good	—	5		—	—	
Outstanding	—	1		—	—	

* Items 7 and 8 were converted to pluses because a *decrease* in the number of times a student "did not respond to another's attempts to interact" or "picked on others" is considered to be an improvement.

average for the control group. Ms. Taylor totaled the number of pluses and subtracted one for Item 3, since there had been a decrease in this behavior. The total gain score for the control group was 6. Despite the fact that two items resulted in zero, Ms. Taylor divided the total gain score by 8, because items 1 through 8 had contributed to the total number of items. She divided 6 by 8 and obtained an average difference score of 0.75.

Ms. Taylor summarized Item 9 by adding the respective numbers of students for both groups who were rated "unsatisfactory," "poor," "so-so," "good," or "outstanding" on level of communication skills for pre- and postcounseling observations. Two students in the counseling group were rated as unsatisfactory, four students were rated as poor, and one student was rated as good in terms of the level of communication skills demonstrated during observations made prior to group counseling. After 6 weeks of group counseling, none of the students in the counseling group received unsatisfactory or poor ratings, one student received a so-so rating, five students received good ratings, and one student received an outstanding rating for the level of communication skills demonstrated during the observations.

Comparing the Control Group to the Counseling Group

The control group was similar, though not identical, to the counseling group prior to the onset of group counseling. Three students were rated unsatisfactory and four students were rated poor on the level of communication skills demonstrated during observations made prior to group counseling. Again, three students were rated unsatisfactory and four students were rated poor on their level of communication skills during observations following six weeks of group counseling.

Interpretation of the Results

The observed total positive shift in the communication skills scores of students in the counseling group was almost 10 times that of the students in the control group. The control group showed slight increases between observation times, but one would expect this to happen by chance.

The counseling and control groups appeared to be relatively similar in communication skills prior to counseling, but after counseling, the counseling-group students improved in eight out of eight (or 100%) of the communication skills. Five of the counseling-group students who had been rated as either unsatisfactory or poor on their level of communication skills prior to counseling (Item 9) were rated as good on these skills after 6 weeks of counseling; the other was rated as outstanding. The student in the counseling group who had been rated as so-so on Item 9 prior to counseling again was rated at that level after 6 weeks of counseling.

The control-group students improved in four out of seven (or 57%) of the communication skills. The ratings for the level of communication skills demonstrated by students in the control group did not improve after the 6 weeks had elapsed.

Examining Results of Individual Students and Specific Items

Applying the Results and Interpretation

The results indicated that a majority (in fact, all) of the students who participated in Ms. Taylor's Peering Up group achieved the goals of the intervention. They used appropriate communication skills to interact with others after small group counseling. Having determined that her group was effective, Ms. Taylor might now review the observational information collected on each student and target students who might benefit from further work on an individual basis. In addition, Ms. Taylor might look at individual items to determine in which areas students in the counseling group made the most and the least gains. For example, the difference scores that were particularly high related to speaking to others, looking at others, and facing others (+12, +15, and +9, respectively). These skills may be easier for middle school students to learn than more abstract skills such as asking questions and giving compliments. Lower gains were made in "smiles at others," "compliments others," and "asks questions." "Picks on others" decreased little. Ms. Taylor may want to revise her group activities based on these results. She also may consider developing an assertiveness training group or classroom unit aimed at teaching middle school students how to be assertive rather than aggressive or passive. Groups or classroom guidance units focused on self-esteem issues and/or respect for others also may be appropriate.

Summary of Evaluation Principles

This example illustrated several important principles that should be kept in mind in all evaluations of school programs. These include the following:

1. The method used to evaluate an intervention should provide the type of information needed to answer the particular evaluation question. This means that a specific evaluation question must be stated. In this case, Ms. Taylor wanted to evaluate changes in communication skills. She used the communication skills she planned to teach in her group as a guide for constructing an instrument and selected a setting (the lunch room) that was conducive to social interaction.
2. Writing a description of what an observer should and should not expect to see (if all goes according to plan) will help determine what items will need to be included in an observation instrument. Including both positively and negatively phrased items reduces the tendency to favor a particular type of response. (See Chapter 3 of the general guide for further discussion about creating your own evaluation instruments.)
3. Try to avoid using value-laden words when writing observation scale items. It is easier and more accurate for observers to record the occurrence of a behavior than to make judgments about what they see. In this case, an item that asked observers to count the number of times a student's posture seemed relaxed and open was dropped because it was too difficult for two observers to agree on when this occurred.
4. Items that are closely and clearly tied to the goals and/or objectives of your interventions will be more informative measures of the effectiveness of the program intervention.
5. Try to limit the items on the instrument to 10 or fewer to make accurate observations as manageable as possible for an observer. Instruments that are straightforward and orderly help observers record their observations easily and more accurately.

6. Objective observers are needed. The less an observer knows about the ultimate purpose of an observation the better. Although the content of the instrument used in this case may have made the goals of the group fairly obvious to the observers, the observers did not know the groups' membership.
7. Observers must be trained on the instrument to be used, with the trainer making sure that the observers understand how the behavior to be observed is being defined. Practice time is needed for the observers to become comfortable with the instrument and to establish interrater reliability (i.e., consistency between their ratings).

Alternative Strategies

Ms. Taylor could conduct a second Peering Up group, using the control group from this evaluation as the counseling group for the new study, and compare the group's relative improvement with that of the first group. If the control group improves, she will have additional evidence of the effectiveness of her Peering Up program.

Multiple Sources of Information

Ms. Taylor also could couple the results obtained from this evaluation with student evaluations of the group experience, teacher ratings of popularity or social skills, and results from homework assignments Ms. Taylor used as reinforcers to group counseling sessions. Just as replicating the success of this group in future studies lends credence to Ms. Taylor's program, use of multiple measures of the success or effectiveness of a program intervention also can strengthen conclusions concerning the success of the overall program. In fact, whenever feasible, multiple measures are desirable. The more types of information Ms. Taylor collects on her interventions, the more support she can compile for the success of her program. For example, Ms. Taylor could have asked teachers to rate the communication skills of each student in both the counseling and control groups. Teachers' perceptions of social behavior sometimes may be influenced by other behaviors, but if positive findings from teachers coincided (or correlated) with positive findings from other sources, Ms. Taylor would have additional evidence of the intervention's effectiveness.

She also might have asked students to keep records of their attempts to make friends, their methods for doing so, and their degree of success. Then she could compile the results to pinpoint strengths and weaknesses in the group intervention for future sessions or groups. This method of data collection, called self-report, requires its own caveats. It would be difficult for Ms. Taylor to verify whether, or to what degree, the information provided by the students was factually accurate. Students' perceptions would be informative, however, especially when coupled with more objective observations. Again, by using one method in conjunction with another, Ms. Taylor could strengthen the results of her evaluations.

Summarizing information collected on group interventions using this and other methods throughout the year will enable Ms. Taylor and Ms. Parrish to determine whether a majority of their students met the goals of group counseling. Areas of needed improvement can be identified, and the overall effectiveness of this program component can be made known.

Cautions Regarding Misinterpretation

Ms. Taylor can report that the students who received the Peering Up group intervention improved their communication skills substantially, whereas the students who did not receive the intervention improved their communication skills relatively little. A majority of the students in the counseling group received the rating of "good" for Item 9 (level of communication skills) following 6 weeks of counseling, whereas none of the students in the control group improved on this item. Unfortunately, Ms. Taylor does not know what aspect of the group counseling experience led to the improvements. It may have been that simply meeting other people through the group improved the social skills of the students involved.

Other Possible Explanations for the Results

Further, the fact that only two observations were conducted makes it difficult to determine how much of the effect on communication skills is attributable to the group intervention and how much reflects fluctuations in how middle school students use those skills from day to day. Perhaps the students whose communication skills improved between the first and second observations were simply having an exceptionally social day. Likewise, it may be that the control students were having an exceptionally isolated day.

Also, as in all program evaluation, there is no guarantee that the results reflect lasting change. Ms. Taylor could conduct a 2- to 4-week follow-up, which would help her determine the degree to which the use of appropriate communication skills was being maintained. Obtaining results similar to her first evaluation would strengthen the conclusion that her Peering Up group is effective in improving the communication skills of seventh graders.

It is always possible that observers somehow influenced the behavior of the students. In this case, however, students in the control group did not seem to reflect such an effect. According to the results of her evaluation, Ms. Taylor's Peering Up group represents an effective intervention for teaching and evaluating appropriate communication skills to seventh-grade students.

4 Vignette Four

Evaluating Classroom Guidance

Rodale High School, which enrolls 800 students in grades 9-12, is located in Gaston, Ohio, a moderately-sized city supported by industrial textile mills, pharmaceutical manufacturing and sales, and telecommunications research companies. Rodale students represent a wide range of socioeconomic backgrounds. About 30% of Rodale's students are black; the rest are white.

The three counselors at Rodale High School want to further the career development of their students. The Ohio state economy is changing. Like those in the rest of the United States, jobs in Ohio are becoming increasingly technical, requiring higher levels of education and expertise. Rodale counselors want to help their students succeed in the future.

Focusing the Evaluation

Leaders in career counseling, such as Dr. Donald Super, believe that career development comprises career orientation, career planning, career exploration, decision making, world-of-work information, and knowledge of preferred occupations. Last year, Rodale's three counselors developed and implemented a career education program in ninth-grade classrooms. This program, called Career 2000, consisted of a series of classroom guidance units and computer exercises using the Ohio Career Information System that are designed to teach career planning, decision making, knowledge of the world of work, and career exploration. Evaluation of the program consisted of surveying student opinions. Ninth graders participating in the Career 2000 program gave it positive ratings.

This year, the three counselors decided to expand their evaluation of the program to determine whether there were positive changes in students' career development. They reviewed the list of standards and indicators for evaluating school counseling programs (see Resource A) and selected Indicator 9.1 ("Evaluation results indicate a majority of students achieve program goals and/or meet specified competencies").

Choosing the Evaluation Method

Strategy for Collecting the Information

The counselors wanted to evaluate whether a majority of the students in the Career 2000 program achieved the career planning, decision-making, world-of-work knowledge, and career exploration competencies specified by the program. They decided to monitor the program by evaluating students' performances in the various classroom guidance activities. Midway into the Career 2000 program, however, the counselors found themselves overwhelmed. First, their monitoring worksheets were extremely time-consuming and confusing to evaluate; the variety of worksheets being used further complicated their attempts. Second, the task of identifying program outcomes —specific career competencies—yielded numerous possibilities. The one thing that became obvious to these counselors was that they were spending inordinate amounts of time trying to identify and select specific competencies in the four goal areas. Their evaluation had become a nightmare.

Evaluating the Appropriateness of a Standardized Instrument

During this time of confusion, one counselor attended a workshop on the use of the Career Development Inventory (CDI) in program evaluation. She reported to her colleagues several advantages of using this instrument to salvage the evaluation of the Career 2000 program. First, because the CDI has subscales that measure the areas of career development targeted in the Career 2000 program, the CDI would eliminate the need to identify actual competencies and the struggle to design worksheets that would measure each of them. Second, the CDI can be scored by computer, thus further reducing the time counselors needed to devote to the evaluation. Third, the CDI is a standardized instrument, which means it provides national norms for a wide range of career competencies. Also, because the validity and reliability of the CDI have been substantiated through research, the counselors could feel reasonably certain that the CDI indeed would measure various attributes of career development consistently. Fourth, the CDI reports results in percentiles. This type of scoring was appealing for several reasons. Counselors typically used percentiles to interpret the results of other standardized instruments used at

Rodale when they discussed student performances with parents. In addition, percentiles would tell counselors the students' standings in their development of actual competencies in terms of the entire population of ninth graders in various parts of the nation who took the CDI.

The CDI was almost too good to be true. The counselors only needed to secure the funds to purchase the CDI package. They called on local business persons who, because of their desire to ensure the availability of a qualified work force in the future, had provided money and/or services for previous programs at Rodale. After hearing the rationale of the Career 2000 program and the appropriateness of the CDI as an evaluation instrument, several business persons gladly agreed to cover the cost of the instrument. The counselors decided to administer the CDI at the conclusion of the Career 2000 program to all 200 ninth-grade students who had participated in order to determine whether a majority of them were in step with ninth graders in other parts of the country who took the CDI.

Studying the Manual and the Instrument

The Career Development Inventory

When the CDI package arrived, the counselors reviewed the manual. The test manual provided information on the norming group, explained and differentiated between the types of scores reported, discussed the test's reliability and validity, and included instructions for administering, scoring, and interpreting the results. The manual said that the CDI was not a timed test. It was divided into two parts: Career Orientation, which would take students 40 minutes to complete, and Knowledge of Preferred Occupations, which would take 25 minutes to complete. The two subscales that measure the competencies taught in the Career 2000 program (career planning, career exploration, decision making, and knowledge of the world of work) are detailed below. (Note: Appreciation is extended to Consulting Psychologists Press, Inc., which provided a complimentary specimen of the Career Development Inventory (CDI) for the preparation of this chapter.)

Career Development Awareness Scale (CDA)

The CDA scale combines the two CDI scales that have been found to be highly interrelated—the Career Planning scale and the Career Exploration scale. The Career Planning scale consists of 20 items in which students report the type and extent of career planning they have engaged in and identify sources for helping them plan. The Career Exploration scale contains 20 items designed to measure attitudes about utilizing and evaluating appropriate sources of information regarding careers. Students are asked to rate various sources of career information and their utility. Developing an attitude toward exploring and evaluating various sources of information is believed to be necessary if students are to obtain needed information in a timely and effective fashion.

Career Development Knowledge and Skills Scale (CDK)

The CDK combines the highly interrelated Decision Making and Knowledge of the World of Work scales. The Decision Making scale consists of 20 sketches; in each situation, students select the appropriate career decisions males and females at various grade levels and in either traditional and nontraditional occupations should make. This scale measures how well students apply what they know to career planning and decision making. The Knowledge of the World of Work scale consists of 20 questions designed to measure students' knowledge of career development tasks, a range of occupations, the structure of occupations, and methods for obtaining and keeping a job.

Type of Scores Reported

Understanding Various Types of Standard Scores to Be Reported

The manual indicated that several types of scores were available. First, *standard scores* represent a transformation of the number of items answered correctly (i.e., raw scores). Raw scores from different subscales are converted so that they can be compared directly. Because the various subscales vary in their length (i.e., number of items), this conversion is necessary before relative strengths and weaknesses can be determined. Students' performances on one subscale thus can be compared with their performance on another subscale. Computerized results, including the mean (or average) for the group's standard scores, are reported. In addition, a standard deviation, which indicates how the scores spread out around their mean, is reported for the group. If a group of scores has a low standard deviation, most of the scores are very close to one another, and the students' scores are fairly similar. A large standard deviation indicates that the range between students' scores is quite wide and that students' scores are fairly dissimilar. (See Chapter 4 in the general guide for a more complete description of mean, variance, and standard deviation.)

Percentile scores also are reported for the CDI subscales. These scores were of particular interest to Rodale's current evaluation of the Career 2000 program because they enabled the counselors to compare individual or group scores to the national population of ninth-grade students. In addition, students and parents were accustomed to receiving percentile scores for other tests administered at Rodale. *Percentile scores* refer to the percentage of the students on which the

CDI was normed who answered the same number or fewer questions correctly as the individual or group in question. A ninth-grade Rodale student, for example, who scored at the 66th percentile on the Career Planning scale scored better than 66% of the students in the norm group taking the CDI. Percentiles should not be confused with *percentage scores,* which indicate the percentage of correct answers on a given test. (See Chapter 4 in the general guide for a more complete description of percentile scores.)

Administering the Career Development Inventory

At the end of the Career 2000 program, all three counselors reread the CDI manual and familiarized themselves with the procedures for test administration. Because the second part of the CDI is not recommended for ninth graders, and because the first part contained the combined subscales selected for the evaluation, the counselors administered only the first part to 200 ninth graders (a total of eight classrooms, with 25 students per classroom).

Standardizing Administration of the Instrument

The counselor who had been conducting the classroom guidance units abstained from test administration because she did not want her presence to influence the results of testing. One of the two counselors not involved in conducting the classroom guidance units administered the CDI to four classrooms one day; the other counselor administered the CDI to four different classrooms the next day. Time blocks of 90 minutes were scheduled for each administration in order to ensure adequate time for instructions and completion of student information. The two test administrators standardized their individual administrations as much as possible by strictly adhering to the procedures outlined in the test manual. This, they hoped, would minimize the influence of individual administration style on the students' answers. Experienced volunteer parents proctored during each administration in order to facilitate the completion of student information, protect the integrity of the test takers, and answer students' questions when appropriate. After all answer sheets had been collected, the volunteer parents examined them for missing student information and stray marks. They combined the 25 answer sheets from each of the eight classrooms, alphabetized them, and sent them to the test publisher for scoring.

Results of the Career Development Inventory

The counselors received computerized score reports for each student and summary scores for the entire group. Shown in Table 4.1 are the means and standard deviations of standard scores and the percentiles for the CDA and CDK subscales for the 200 ninth-grade students participating in the Career 2000 program.

Understanding Standard Scores

In the national norming group, standard scores for all subscales of the CDI have a mean of 100 and a standard deviation of 20. The mean standard score represents the score of the typical ninth grader. The mean CDA standard score scale for the 200 ninth-graders participating in the Career 2000 program was 102, two points higher than the mean of all CDI standard scores in the national norm group. The standard deviation on the CDA subscale for the Rodale students, 23, was slightly higher than the standard deviation of 20 found for the national norm group. This indicated that the range of the Rodale students' scores was similar to that of the norm group. Rodale's ninth graders' mean standard score for the CDA placed them at the 64th percentile nationally. This score indicates that Rodale's ninth graders answered more items on the scale correctly than did 64% of the entire population of ninth graders who took the CDI.

The group mean for the CDK scale was 106, six points higher than the national norm group mean of 100. The standard deviation obtained for the Rodale ninth graders' standard scores was 21. The Rodale group scored at the 66th percentile on this scale, indicating that Rodale's students answered more answers correctly than 66% of the entire population of ninth graders on whom the CDI was normed.

Interpretation of the Results

Standard scores for the CDA subscale that fall much below the mean of 100 indicate a need to stimulate a sense of the importance of systematic career planning. Standard scores that fall close to or above the mean indicate a readiness to move further in the planning and exploration processes. The 64th-percentile ranking indicates that Rodale's ninth graders answered more items correctly on the CDA subscale than would be considered average; the average for the norm group is the 50th percentile of scores earned by the population of ninth-grade students who took the CDI. Rodale's students appear to be ready to move further in their development of career planning and career exploration competencies.

TABLE 4.1 Score Reports for the CDA and CDK

Scale	Mean Standard Score	Standard Deviation	National Percentile
CDA ($n = 200$)	102	23	64
CDK ($n = 200$)	106	21	66

Comparing Results to Norm Group Scores

The standard deviation of the standard scores on the CDA for the Rodale students indicated that there was a slightly greater spread of Rodale students' scores than was found in the population at large. This is to be expected, because there were only 200 Rodale students and more than 1,000 ninth-grade students in the norming group. The mean of a large group, such as the CDI norm group, tends to be less affected by extreme scores because extreme scores constitute a smaller part of a large sample. Conversely, the mean of a smaller group, like the Rodale group, will be more affected by extreme scores because the former is based on fewer scores. The counselors at Rodale might want to examine individual scores to identify students who may require individual help in developing career planning competencies.

A mean standard score of 100 or better on the CDK subscale indicates (a) an ability to make independent career decisions, and (b) an appropriate knowledge of various occupations and their structure. The Rodale students' mean standard score of 106 suggested that this group of students have developed a slightly better than average competence in knowledge and skill. A percentile score of 66 demonstrates that Rodale's students have achieved this goal of the program and are ready to move further in developing decision-making skills and a world-of-work knowledge base.

As a group, the 200 ninth-grade students participating in Rodale's Career 2000 program achieved the goals of the program. They appeared to be slightly better than the average ninth-grader in career planning, obtaining and evaluating sources of career information, applying knowledge to decision making, and understanding the structure of the world of work.

Applying the Results and Interpretation

The purpose of this year's evaluation study was to obtain information that would enable counselors at Rodale to determine whether a majority of the students in the Career 2000 program achieved targeted career competencies. After examination of the mean standard scores and percentile scores for each of the selected subscales, the counselors concluded that the group achieved the specified student competencies of the Career 2000 program.

Examining Results of Individual Students and Specific Items

The counselors were aware that the group scores did not identify which students failed to achieve the student competencies. Group scores also do not point to the items students answered correctly and incorrectly most often. The counselors' next task was to identify who did not score at or above the 50th percentile on either subscale, so that these students could be targeted for additional help.

Counselors also can examine one other type of score provided by the computerized service. Frequency data can be used to indicate the number of students who choose each possible answer for each question. This type of report could reveal which items were easy and which were hard for the Rodale students. Examining frequency responses could help Rodale's counselors identify areas of strengths and areas of needed improvement in the Career 2000 program.

Summary of Evaluation Principles

This example illustrated several important principles that should be kept in mind in all evaluations of school programs. These are as follows:

1. When selecting an evaluation method, try to think in terms of the type of information you will need to answer the evaluation question. In this case, counselors wanted to know how their students stood in terms of a national norm; therefore, a standardized instrument that reported national norms was desirable.
2. Select an instrument that seems to be a valid measure of your program goals. In this case, the CDI included scales that measured the specific competencies covered by the Career 2000 program.
3. A test manual provides valuable information that warrants careful study. The CDI manual described the various types of scores that were available and how to interpret the results in a meaningful way. Just as important, the manual described procedures for standardized administration of the instrument.
4. When more than one person will be involved in administering an instrument, it is best to try to standardize the administration in order to protect the validity of the study. In this case, the two counselors were careful to adhere to the manual during test administration and explained to experienced volunteer parents what assistance to students was or was not appropriate.
5. Evaluation results are helpful to the extent that the results are understood by students, parents, and teachers. The counselors planned to use percentile scores in reporting results because this type of score was familiar to the Rodale community.

Other Methods of Collecting Information

Alternative Strategies

Counselors turned to the CDI because of their difficulties in using classroom worksheets as evaluation instruments. One consideration for the future use of the CDI is the cost involved in buying and scoring the instrument. Counselors must balance cost against their desire for a reliable and valid measure of student competencies and their interest in knowing Rodale students' national standing in regard to their career development. The counselors may want to spend some time revising a few of their worksheets for next year's ninth graders. They could concentrate on devising checklists that measure competencies of particular interest.

Other potential indicators of the effectiveness of the career counseling program include increased use of career resource materials and requests for appointments to discuss career plans. The counselors may want to document these and other behaviors related to career development.

Cautions Regarding Misinterpretations

Adding a Pretest

Although the results obtained in this case certainly warrant the continuation of the Career 2000 program, it would be a mistake to assume that the program alone is responsible for them. Several caveats must be considered. First, there is no measure of how these ninth graders stood in terms of the national norms prior to the Career 2000 program; therefore, it is difficult to ascertain whether or not they actually improved. Students may have had similar scores before participating in the Career 2000 program. The counselors may want to include a pretest and posttest of all Rodale students (or a random sample of students) in next year's program. If they want an even more rigorous test of the Career 2000 program, they may include a control group in their evaluation (see Chapter 3).

Other Possible Explanations for the Results

Without pretest results, it is impossible to say what, if any, impact the Career 2000 program had on Rodale students' CDI scores. Many other factors influence students' career development. Developmental changes in cognition would have influenced students' attitudes toward career planning and exploration, as well as their ability to think abstractly about decisions. Life experiences outside the academic curriculum, such as participation in clubs, sports, or the Jaycees, also may have influenced the development of students' career competence. Perhaps students began working their first part-time jobs the same semester that the program began. Any of these changes probably would have an effect on competencies related to career development.

Which aspects or combination of aspects of the program resulted in Rodale ninth graders achieving an above-average national standing is unclear; however, a program that is not unwieldy to deliver or to evaluate and does seem to produce positive results probably should not be altered unnecessarily. Assessing students prior to and at the conclusion of the Career 2000 program and using a control group in next year's program will help determine actual change in specified career competencies. Collecting information on this group next year (as 10th graders) will enable the counselors to evaluate the effects of the Career 2000 program over time. For now, however, Rodale High School counselors seem to have a good thing going.

5

Vignette Five

Assessing Parents' Opinions of the Overall Program

Northside High School is located in Oxford, a city of 190,000 in central Indiana. Northside, one of three high schools in the city school system, enrolls 2,000 students in grades 9-12. It offers a typical comprehensive high school curriculum in addition to remedial courses, vocational education, and advanced courses for academically talented students. Students are bused to Northside from three distinct neighborhoods: one that is favored by employees of manufacturing firms in the city (Glen Arbor), one that is populated by professors at a local university and other professionals (Deer Lake), and a third that is composed of subsidized housing and includes several recent immigrant groups (Royal Oak). Northside is ethnically as well as socioeconomically diverse.

The school counseling department at Northside includes four counselors and two full-time support staff who collectively serve as the department's receptionist, secretary, and registrar. A career and educational resource room contains numerous written and visual materials; it also houses a computerized program to assist students' educational and career planning.

Focusing the Evaluation

The activity level in the counseling office and resource room suggests that students freely seek out information and services offered by the four school counselors. The counselors have worked deliberately to establish a comprehensive program and a favorable reputation over the last few years. In particular, they wanted students to know that they provide personal and interpersonal counseling as well as assistance with educational and career planning. Recent evaluations by students, teachers, and administrators indicated that they have succeeded for the most part.

The counselors, however, are aware that their "consumers" include at least one other group—parents—and they want to target that group this year. This plan is in line with Indicator 9.2 ("Evaluation results indicate that a majority of students, parents, teachers, and administrators hold favorable opinions of the school counseling program").

The counselors have made some efforts to reach parents and inform them of the positive changes in the program. They have sent notices concerning workshops (e.g., financial aid) home via students, described their program at schoolwide parent-teacher meetings, and solicited parent volunteers to serve on the school advisory committee. They are aware, however, that these efforts are no guarantee that all (or a substantial proportion of) parents have been reached. The planned evaluation should help counselors learn how successful their previous efforts have been.

Strategy for Collecting Information

At a school counseling advisory committee meeting, the counselors announced their evaluation plan and led a brainstorming session about possible procedures. Committee members identified several approaches, including a questionnaire, interviews, and focus groups. During discussion, the counselors realized they preferred personal contacts with parents, both for purposes of the evaluation and for public relations. They also wanted to allow parents to respond to follow-up questions and to feel free to make unsolicited comments. Focus groups would allow in-depth discussion about the counseling program but would require parents to attend scheduled meetings. Advisory committee members suggested this might prove difficult, because almost all parents of Northside students worked. Face-to-face interviews presented similar problems. A telephone survey seemed a viable and efficient alternative. Committee members set themselves the task of creating a structured interview protocol and soliciting volunteer interviewers.

Choosing Appropriate Interviewers

Clearly, counselors could not act as interviewers. Despite their genuine interest in parents' opinions, they were too invested in the results of the survey to be objective. Parents on the school advisory committee agreed to solicit parent volunteers to serve as interviewers. Counselors took on the task of designing a structured interview protocol.

Defining the Content of the Interview

Northside's comprehensive school counseling program includes services targeted at all four competency areas that typically compose a comprehensive program (i.e., educational, career, personal, and social development; see Indicator 6.3). The counselors wanted the interview questions to cover all four areas. When considering survey procedures, they realized that the interview needed to be brief and that they should avoid using counseling vocabulary with which the public might not be familiar.

Creating the Interview Protocol and Script

The counselors presented their first draft of the interview protocol to the school advisory committee at the next meeting. Committee members reviewed the wording and content of the protocol. Following discussion, a final interview protocol and script were completed (see Figure 5.1). Committee members reported that 10 parents had volunteered to serve as interviewers. A 2-hour training session was scheduled for the following week.

Selecting a Random Sample of Parents

In the meantime, counselors began to identify the parents who would be interviewed. They wanted to include parents of students in all four grades and from all three neighborhoods served by Northside. Thus they needed a random sample of the parents of the entire student body. To guide their selection of a representative sample, the counselors consulted a book on sampling procedures (e.g., Jaeger, *Sampling in Education and the Social Sciences;* see Resource B). There they found a chart for determining how large their sample should be (i.e., how many parents in the total population of parents should be interviewed). The chart offered the following choices:

Sample size when the population totals:	1,000	10,000
To be 80% confident of the results with no more than a 5% error rate:	141	162
To be 95% confident of the results with no more than a 5% error rate:	278	370
To be 80% confident of the results with no more than a 10% error rate:	40	41
To be 95% confident of the results with no more than a 10% error rate:	88	96

Although the counselors valued accuracy (i.e., higher confidence percentage, lower error rate), they also had to be realistic about the

Circle one: Interviewer: _____

   1. Glen Arbor
   2. Deer Lake
   3. Royal Oak

Parent Interview Protocol

May I speak with Mr. , Ms. , Mr. or Mrs. _____, ?

Mr./Ms./Mrs. _____, I am a parent volunteer for the counseling department at Northside High School. Northside school counselors have asked us to help them evaluate their program by asking a select group of parents about their contacts with the counseling department. The questions are brief, and it will take about 15 minutes to answer all of them. We are interested in your honest and candid answers. Your answers will be kept completely confidential and anonymous. I will record your answers on a form; no identifying information, such as your name, will be recorded on the form. Would you be willing to participate in our survey?

(If parent answers, NO, say "Thanks, anyway." Record any reason the parent gives about declining to participate.)

(If parent answers YES, proceed with interview questions below.)

(Remember: Circle answers provided. Write responses to follow-up and open-ended questions using the parent's words and as completely as possible. Also write in any comments made about the structured questions.)

Interview Questions

Background Information

1. First, do you have a SON or a DAUGHTER enrolled at Northside?
   (NOTE: Use the parent's response in wording the following questions.)
2. Is your son/daughter in the 9th, 10th, 11th, or 12th grade at Northside?

    9   10   11   12

3. Are you aware that a counselor in your son's/daughter's school has been assigned to assist him/her?

    YES   NO

    Comments:

4. Do you know the name of your son's/daughter's school counselor?

    YES   NO

    Comments:

5. To your knowledge, has your son/daughter had contact with the counselor?

    YES   NO

    Comments:

6. Have you had contact with the counselor?

    YES   NO

    Comments:

Counseling Services and Resources

I am now going to read a list of services and resources provided as part of the Northside counseling program. For each, we want to know two things: (1) Are you aware that each service is offered? (2) If you are aware of that service, would you rate the service as excellent, good, fair, or poor? You may add any comments you wish to clarify your answers. Any questions?

Figure 5.1. Interview Protocol

7. First, are you aware that the Northside counseling department has a Resource Room with information on colleges and technical/vocational schools, and information on a variety of careers?

                    YES   NO

(If yes) Do you believe the Resource Room is excellent, good, fair, or poor? (Circle answer)

    EXCELLENT   GOOD   FAIR   POOR

Are you aware that the Northside counseling program offers your son/daughter help with

    Educational

8. Selecting his/her high school courses at Northside?

                    YES   NO

(If yes) Do you believe this service is

    EXCELLENT   GOOD   FAIR   POOR

9. Improving study skills?

                    YES   NO

(If yes) Do you believe this service is

    EXCELLENT   GOOD   FAIR   POOR

10. Applying for admission to college and/or technical/vocational schools?

                    YES   NO

(If yes) Do you believe this service is

    EXCELLENT   GOOD   FAIR   POOR

11. Applying for financial aid to cover college and/or technical/vocational schools' expenses?

                    YES   NO

(If yes) Do you believe this service is

    EXCELLENT   GOOD   FAIR   POOR

    Career

12. Choosing a career?

                    YES   NO

(If yes) Do you believe this service is

    EXCELLENT   GOOD   FAIR   POOR

13. Planning for that career?

                    YES   NO

(If yes) Do you believe this service is

    EXCELLENT   GOOD   FAIR   POOR

14. Completing job applications, writing a resume, and practicing for job interviews?

                    YES   NO

(If yes) Do you believe this service is

    EXCELLENT   GOOD   FAIR   POOR

    Personal

15. Dealing with personal issues, such as coping with the pressures of being an adolescent and growing up?

                    YES   NO

(If yes) Do you believe this service is

    EXCELLENT   GOOD   FAIR   POOR

Social

16. Improving relationships with others, including peers, teachers, family members, and other adults?

                YES   NO

(If yes) Do you believe this service is

    EXCELLENT   GOOD   FAIR   POOR

Parent Referrals

For which of the following would you recommend that your son/daughter consult with his/her counselor?

17. Educational planning

                YES   NO

18. Career planning

                YES   NO

19. Personal issues

                YES   NO

20. Interpersonal (relations) issues

                YES   NO

21. Would you be willing to share the reasons for your responses concerning these recommendations with your son/daughter?

Closing Questions

The last three questions ask for your general opinions about the Northside counseling program.

22. Overall, how would you rate the counseling program at Northside?

    EXCELLENT   GOOD   FAIR   POOR

23. In your opinion, what are the strengths of the counseling program at Northside?

24. What suggestions do you have for improving the counseling program at Northside?

25. We'd appreciate any final comments.

    I really appreciate your time and your candid answers to these questions. I'm sure your responses will be very helpful to the counselors. Goodbye.

Figure 5.1. Continued

number of interviews that could be conducted. The last alternative (95% confident, 10% error rate) seemed a good compromise. They estimated a sample size of 100 parents, including a few extras as backups in the event of wrong numbers or similar problems. (The chart included populations of 1,000 and 10,000, but not 2,000, the total student body at Northside, so the counselors had to estimate the sample size.)

    The next task was to select 100 parents randomly to be interviewed. Because the counselors wanted to select 100 parents out of 2,000, it appeared that they could begin with a random name on a list and then pick every 20th name on the list (2,000 ÷ 100 = 20). To get the number for the first random name, the counselors decided to use the head counselor's birthday. If the birthday date was less than 20, they could use that number; if it was 21 or over, they would divide it in half and round up. Because the head counselor's birthday was January 27, they arrived at 14 as their first random number (27 ÷ 2 = 13.5, which rounds up to 14). (This procedure is called "linear systematic sampling.")

Next, the counselors went to an alphabetical computer listing of all Northside students. This combined list (as opposed to a list by grade level) was necessary to get a random sample that would include each grade level and each neighborhood. They found the 14th name on the list and then went through the list to identify every 20th name. Finally, they printed a copy of the list of 100 parents that included names, addresses, and phone numbers. Addresses were listed so that the interviewers could indicate on the answer form the parents' neighborhood; in this way, answers from each neighborhood could be compared. Copies of the lists were prepared so that they could be distributed to the volunteer interviewers at the training session.

Training the Interviewers

The training session covered basic interviewing skills and a thorough review of the interview questions and interview procedure. This training was necessary for the following reasons:

- to acquaint volunteer interviewers with the purpose of the evaluation
- to establish mutual agreement about the meaning of the interview questions (including definitions of services such as career planning, personal counseling, etc.)
- to give volunteers ample opportunity to become familiar (and comfortable) with the script and protocol
- to allow volunteers to practice recording parents' responses
- to ensure consistency in the conduct of the interviews
- to identify and plan responses for atypical situations (e.g., parents who would answer only a few questions, parents who did not speak English, students who lived with their grandparents)

During the training exercises, volunteers (practicing in dyads) offered several useful suggestions, such as keeping a tally of wrong phone numbers and persons who chose not to respond and jotting down reasons persons gave for declining to participate. At the conclusion of the training session, each of the 10 volunteers was assigned the names of 10 parents from the sample.

Results of the Interviews

Two weeks later, the phone volunteers returned a total of 92 completed interview protocols. This total number was a sufficient sample size according to the confidence level the counselors had selected (see above). The school counseling advisory committee members tallied the responses during a special meeting.

Determining the Representativeness of the Respondents

First, responses to questions 1 and 2 were tabulated, so that committee members could determine how closely the students of interviewed parents resembled the Northside student body. The percentage of parents who had daughters at Northside (Question 1) was found to be $(58 \div 92) \times 100 = (0.6304) \times (100) = 63.04 = 63\%$. This percentage meant that the sample included a higher percentage of females than there were in the total student population at Northside (52%). Responses to question 2 indicated the following grade-level distribution: grade 9, 27%; grade 10, 27%; grade 11, 24%; and grade 12, 22%. These percentages compared favorably to the percentages of students in each grade level at Northside. Thus, based on the responses to questions 1 and 2, the sample was judged to be fairly representative of Northside students, although males were underrepresented somewhat.

Next, the interview protocols were separated into neighborhood groups. This sorting indicated that 28 Glen Arbor (Neighborhood 1), 33 Deer Lake (Neighborhood 2), and 31 Royal Oak (Neighborhood 3) parents had been interviewed. Because the three neighborhoods were represented fairly equally in the total student population, the interview sample seemed representative.

Determining Percentages of Responses

For the remaining questions, committee members tabulated the results separately for each neighborhood group. Response counts for each yes/no question were converted to percentages; each response count was divided by the total number of responses for that neighborhood, the resulting fraction was multiplied by 100, and then the percentage was rounded to a whole number. For example, the percentage of Glen Arbor parents who were aware of the resource room (Question 7) was found to be $(12 \div 28) \times 100 = (0.4286) \times (100) = 42.86 = 43\%$.

Determining Mean Ratings on Likert Scales

Opinion responses about specific services (questions 7 through 16) were converted to a Likert rating scale: "Excellent" responses were given 4 points; "good" responses, 3 points; "fair" responses, 2 points; and "poor" responses, 1 point. (See Chapter 3 in the general guide for a further explanation of Likert rating scales.) The resulting ratings were totaled and averaged for each question, with the average rounded off to one decimal point. For example, the average (mean) rating for Question 7 by Glen Arbor parents (Neighborhood 1) was found to be (32 ÷ 11)= 2.90 = 3.0. In other words, a total of 32 points was given in the ratings; the number of Glen Arbor parents who answered "yes" and then rated the item was 11. The 11 parents' average rating for Question 7 was 3.0.

Questions 3 through 6 required a "yes" or "no" response. Committee members found the following percentages of "yes" responses:

Question	Neighborhood 1	Neighborhood 2	Neighborhood 3
3	82%	100%	100%
4	51%	98%	92%
5	65%	98%	98%
6	42%	90%	94%

These results suggested that most parents were aware that their son or daughter had been assigned a counselor and that they knew who their child's counselor was. Parents in Glen Arbor (Neighborhood 1) reported less contact with school counselors for themselves and for their children than did parents in Deer Park (Neighborhood 2) and Royal Oak (Neighborhood 3).

Responses to questions 7 through 16 provided two sources of information: percentages of parents who were aware of specific counseling services, and parents' ratings of those services. The overall rating of services (Question 21) was added to this table because of its relevance to the other items (see Table 5.1).

These results suggested that parents in Glen Arbor (Neighborhood 1) were less aware of Northside's counseling services than were parents in the other two neighborhoods. Glen Arbor parents also gave these services the lowest ratings. In general, all parents seemed more aware of (and were more favorable about) counseling services for educational development than for career, personal, or social development.

Responses to questions 17 through 20 indicated parents' willingness to refer their son or daughter for counseling services. Percentages of "yes" responses to these questions were as follows:

Question	Neighborhood 1	Neighborhood 2	Neighborhood 3
17	50%	100%	80%
18	50%	90%	80%
19	30%	30%	70%
20	40%	30%	70%

These results suggested that parents in Glen Arbor (Neighborhood 1) were less likely than other parents to recommend that their son or daughter consult with a counselor. In general, all parents seemed more willing to refer their son or daughter for counseling for educational and career issues than for personal or interpersonal (social) issues.

TABLE 5.1 Parents' Responses to Questions 7 Through 16

Subject/Question	Neighborhood 1 Yes %	Rating	Neighborhood 2 Yes %	Rating	Neighborhood 3 Yes %	Rating
Resource Room						
7	43	3.0	100	3.8	82	3.2
Educational						
8	95	3.0	100	3.8	100	3.6
9	62	2.7	90	3.5	75	3.5
10	55	2.8	100	3.7	80	3.2
11	61	2.6	100	3.3	88	3.5
Career						
12	48	2.6	80	3.2	82	3.2
13	43	2.8	80	3.2	82	3.2
14	30	2.8	50	3.0	60	3.0
Personal						
15	40	2.8	80	3.0	90	3.5
Social						
16	50	2.8	80	3.0	90	3.5
Overall						
21		2.8		3.5		3.5

Categorizing Responses to Open-Ended Questions

Responses to questions 22 and 23, open-ended inquiries about the counseling program, were read by two parents on the committee. The two questions summarized parents' responses into the categories shown in Table 5.2.

Finally, comments in response to Question 24 and earlier questions were summarized by two other committee members. These comments included compliments and complaints; they primarily were accounts of a parent's individual contact with the counseling program. In general, this feedback paralleled the categories of strengths and suggestions for improvement reported for earlier questions.

Comparing Responses From Each Neighborhood

Interpretation of the Results

Committee members made the following general conclusions based on the results of the parent interviews:

1. Parents in Glen Arbor were less informed about the variety of counseling services than were parents in Deer Lake and Royal Oak. In particular, they were unaware of the availability of information on postsecondary technical/vocational schools and financial aid oppor-

Table 5.2 Summarized Responses of Parents to Questions 22 and 23

Question 22: Strengths of the counseling program Category	Number (Frequency)
Availability of materials on variety of colleges	72
Financial aid workshops for parents and students	51
Counselors available for student appointments	40
Counselors available for parent conferences	32
Other (e.g., extended help to students, advocate for students)	20

Question 23: Suggestions for improvement Category	Number (Frequency)
Parent newsletter about college and financial aid applications, deadlines	32
Work with all students, not just college bound	20
More after-school appointment times for parents	12
Other	6

tunities for students attending those schools. These parents also did not know that job search strategies were part of Northside's counseling services.

2. Deer Lake parents seemed well aware of the variety of counseling services offered at Northside; most had been in direct contact with their son or daughter's counselor. These parents reported favorable opinions of the counseling services, especially those related to educational development. They indicated a greater willingness to refer their son or daughter to a Northside counselor for educational and/or career planning than for personal, social, or family issues.

3. Royal Oak parents reported awareness of and favorable opinions of the variety of counseling services at Northside. Most had been in direct contact with their son or daughter's counselor, were satisfied with those contacts, and were apt to refer their son or daughter to the counselor for a wide range of counseling issues. These parents, however, were relatively uninformed about help with job search strategies and resources related to postsecondary technical/vocational schools (including financial aid). During the interviews, a number of these parents expressed appreciation for a counselor's efforts to encourage their son or daughter to attend college and in helping them obtain financial aid.

4. In general, all parents seemed to be more aware of and more favorable about counseling services targeted at educational planning than services meant to enhance career, personal, and social development. They were more willing to refer their son or daughter for educational and career issues than for personal or interpersonal (social) issues.

Planning Changes Based on Results

Applying the Results and Interpretation

Although the parent interviews suggested generally favorable opinions of the counseling program, it was clear that additional efforts were needed. Apparently, there was a need to inform parents of counseling services targeted toward students' personal and social development, assistance with job search strategies, and resources related to postsecondary opportunities other than four-year colleges. Particular attention needed to be given to Glen Arbor parents.

The school counseling advisory committee planned to spend several future meetings discussing what changes or additional efforts they could make, including the parent newsletter suggested by a number of the parents who were interviewed. The results also suggested that committee members might want to consider ways to explore parents' ideas about the appropriate functions of the counseling program and the contrasts between parents' opinions of counseling services and the opinions of students and teachers (from previous evaluations).

Summary of Evaluation Principles

This example illustrated several important principles that should be kept in mind when conducting similar evaluations. These principles include the following:

1. Interviews should be conducted by persons who have little or no investment in the results. Interviewers must maintain objectivity in the way they ask questions, record responses, and interact with interviewees. In this case, parents rather than counselors were preferable as interviewers. Similarly, responses to open-ended questions and parents' comments were categorized by committee members other than the counselors. (See Chapter 3 in the general guide for further discussion of interviews as an evaluation method.) In other evaluations, counselors may desire student interviews. To obtain honest answers, students probably should be interviewed by persons who *aren't* directly associated with the school (e.g., counselors, teachers) or their peers and family (e.g., parents). Outside interviewers would be needed especially for topics such as drug use and sexual behavior. Possible outside interviewers include faculty and/or students from a nearby postsecondary institution and members of a community service club.
2. A standardized protocol for interviews is preferable. In this case, counselors devised a script and training sessions to ensure consistency in the conduct of the interviews and the recording of responses. Such standardization is necessary to obtain valid results.
3. Interview questions, like questionnaire items, may be open ended or highly structured. Questions that have a standard response format

(e.g., yes/no; excellent, good, fair, or poor) provide responses that are relatively easy to tally, compare, and interpret; they also may be easier to answer. Open-ended questions provide more detailed and individual answers; they also are harder to summarize accurately. Counselors need to consider exactly what information is desired and then construct questions that will provide that information in the most economical and feasible way.

4. Interview questions should be worded clearly and free of jargon. Pilot testing is helpful, because it is often difficult to anticipate what words or phrases will confuse persons being interviewed.
5. The overall length of an interview must be realistic. A feasible range is 5 to 15 minutes.
6. Parents (and students, teachers, etc.) are more likely to give honest answers if their responses are kept confidential. If possible, anonymous responses are preferred.

Other Methods of Collecting Information

Alternative Strategies

The counselors in this example decided to conduct interviews because they wanted to have personal contacts with parents and to allow follow-up questions to parents' initial responses. They did not use face-to-face interviews or focus groups because of possible scheduling problems. The latter two strategies could have provided greater depth and open discussions, but they also may have limited the number of parents who could be invited to participate.

A written questionnaire (similar to the interview protocol questions) also could have been used. This strategy would have allowed a larger sample of parents for the same amount of time. It would have required funds for printing, supplies, and postage, however, and it would not provide a guarantee that sampled parents would have responded in reasonable numbers.

Cautions Regarding Misinterpretation

Results of the parent interviews are limited by the confidence level associated with the sample size (see previous chart). In addition, group comparisons were based on small numbers of parents in some cases. For example, 43%—or 11—Glen Arbor parents were aware of the resource room. This means that the 3.0 average rating for the resource room was based on individual ratings of only 11 parents in that neighborhood.

Interpretation of the results also must reflect the wording of the questions. For example, parents were asked to rate counseling services offered at Northside; they did not indicate their opinions about the relative importance of these services.

Later, the school advisory committee might decide they want overall ratings for the entire sample of parents. They will not be able to average the percentages and mean ratings of the three neighborhoods to get an overall average, unless the committee has up-to-date information on the sizes of the parent populations in these neighborhoods. Otherwise, the answer of each individual in the total sample must be entered to get accurate percentages and means for the total group.

6 Vignette Six

Surveying Teachers' Opinions of Selected Program Components

Built in the early 1980s, McKinley Elementary School enrolls 365 children in grades K-5. It draws students from all sections of Midville, Colorado, a city of 20,000 that is supported by a variety of light industries and agricultural sales and processing. Students are bused to McKinley from three distinct neighborhoods in Midville: one that is favored by assembly line workers in a farm implement factory, one favored by midlevel management personnel who commute an hour to their jobs in a large Colorado city, and a third composed of subsidized housing for low-income renters. McKinley is racially as well as socioeconomically diverse. About 40% of the school's pupils are black; the rest are white.

June Snow, principal of McKinley, is proud of the accomplishments of her staff of 16 teachers, a school counselor, and a media specialist. In her five years as principal, she has seen her school's enrollment and staff grow steadily. She believes McKinley's professionals are committed to high-quality education, to McKinley, and to the children they serve. She prides herself in working with her teachers and other professionals to improve the effectiveness of the school through a continuing program of selective, focused evaluation. Because McKinley's staff regard Ms. Snow as fair and supportive, they willingly participate in ongoing program evaluation.

At a beginning-of-the-year meeting involving all professionals employed at McKinley, the teachers and school counselor agreed that the main focus of evaluation this year would be the school's counseling program. Ms. Snow and the teachers made certain that Mr. Hanna, the school counselor, knew that they were not evaluating him so much as the counseling program itself. Of course, in a small school with only one counselor, the person and the program are to some extent inseparable. The counselor agreed that he would benefit from an evaluation of his program, and he was interested in learning the strengths and weaknesses of his program as well as those of his own functioning as a counselor. If he could do his job better, he wanted to find out how.

Three McKinley teachers agreed to work with Ms. Snow in evaluating the school's counseling program. Ms. Carlyle, a first-grade teacher, often depended on the counselor to help students adjust to the rigors of life in a structured classroom. Ms. Joyner sometimes sought help from the counselor in dealing with her overactive fifth graders. And Mr. Simms, in his second year of teaching the third grade, relied on the counselor to help him structure instructional modules that were appropriate to his students' differing developmental levels. All three teachers recognized the value of an effective school counseling program and were willing to devote a little extra time if the program could be made more effective.

Focusing the Evaluation

A school counseling program is complex. Evaluating an entire program takes time and money, both of which were in short supply at McKinley. The three teachers wondered which program components they should focus on in their evaluation. Like most elementary counselors, Mr. Hanna provided classroom guidance, individual and small group counseling, and consultation for teachers and parents. He routinely collected evaluations from the students who participated in his small counseling groups and from those who saw him for individual counseling, but he had not formally evaluated his classroom guidance or consultation activities. Ms. Snow and the three teachers decided that an appropriate focus for their evaluation would be teachers' opinions of the counseling services they observed or received themselves: classroom guidance and consultation. Reviewing the list of standards and indicators for school counseling programs during a planning session, they selected Indicator 9.4 ("Evaluation results indicate that teachers believe counselors are responsive, competent, available, and collaborative").

Strategy for Collecting Information

The evaluation team considered several ways to assess Indicator 9.4. It was clear from the statement of the indicator that they had to determine the judgments of their fellow teachers. They thought about face-to-face interviews with a few teachers right after school as one possibility, but rejected the idea because they realized that the judgments of a few teachers might not reflect those of all teachers at McKinley. Also, interviews conducted right after school had several drawbacks: (a) the time might be inconvenient for some teachers; (b) after a long day in the classroom, teachers would be tired and not much interested in being interviewed; and (c) although the results of interviews can be kept confidential, interviews aren't anonymous (therefore, teachers might be reluctant to express their views of the counseling program freely).

Comparing Interviews and Surveys

Holding a meeting of all teachers was rejected for many of the same reasons, as well as some others. Finding a convenient time for everyone would be difficult. A meeting during the school day would take teachers out of their classrooms, and a meeting after school would catch teachers when they were tired. In addition, some teachers might be reluctant to speak up in a meeting, and others might dominate the discussion so that the views of only a few would be heard. There would be no guarantee that the views of these few would reflect the views of all teachers.

After rejecting these alternatives, the team settled on the idea of sending a questionnaire to all 13 McKinley teachers who weren't on the evaluation team, in addition to completing a questionnaire themselves. Teachers presumably would feel free to express their views on an anonymous questionnaire. Judgments could be collected from all teachers at McKinley, not just a few. Teachers could complete the questionnaire at a time of their own choosing, making the response task more convenient.

Defining the Goals of the Evaluation

The evaluation team met several times to write items for the questionnaire. They used the adjectives listed in Indicator 9.4 (i.e., *responsive, competent, available,* and *collaborative*) and the two counseling activities they had identified (i.e., classroom guidance and consultation) to guide the content of their items. At least one statement was written to reflect each dimension (adjective) named in the indicator. The team included more statements pertaining to competence than any of the other dimensions; they recognized that competence is a broad category, and they wanted to secure information on various aspects of competence related to classroom guidance and consultation. The final list included the following distribution of items: responsiveness, one item; competence, six items; availability, two items; and collaboration, one item.

Writing Items for a Likert Scale

Next, the team had to chose the response format for the items. They found a format in a program evaluation book that appeared useful and appropriate. A Likert scale would allow teachers to indicate the degree to which they agreed or disagreed with each evaluative statement. The program evaluation book explained that both positive and negative items were needed when using a Likert scale. A balance of positive and negative statements was needed because some people tend to agree with all items on a long list containing only positive statements, just out of habit. (This tendency to agree with positive statements, as discussed earlier, is called a response set.) According to the book, this problem could be a major source of invalid results when Likert scales are used, but it could be avoided easily by writing a mixture of positive and negative statements. (See Chapter 3 of the general guide for a further explanation of Likert scales.)

The team decided to adopt this scale format and changed the wording of four items to make them negative statements. They also added a statement at the end inviting teachers to provide any comments they chose concerning the overall quality of the school counseling program. The final questionnaire is presented in Figure 6.1.

Determining the Procedure

At the next regularly scheduled staff meeting Ms. Snow asked Ms. Carlyle to explain what the evaluation team recommended, and she secured the agreement of all McKinley teachers to complete a questionnaire and return it to Ms. Carlyle within 1 week. Teachers were to call on a member of the evaluation team for clarification if they had any questions about the content of the questionnaire. Questionnaires would be distributed to teachers in large manila envelopes by placing them in the teachers' mailboxes in the school office. Teachers would use the same (unmarked) envelopes to return the questionnaire.

Results of the Survey Questionnaires

Within 1 week, each teacher, including the three on the evaluation team, had left a completed questionnaire in Ms. Carlyle's mailbox. Ms. Carlyle and Mr. Simms worked together to summarize the teachers' questionnaire responses. They began by counting the number of teachers who had selected each response to each of the 10 statements. Then, to make the results easier to understand, they

McKinley Elementary School
Counseling Program Evaluation Questionnaire

DIRECTIONS: Please mark the one column after each of the following statements that best describes your own judgment about the statement. Circle the answer that matches your judgment:

SA	Strongly Agree
A	Agree
U	Uncertain
D	Disagree
SD	Strongly Disagree

Be certain that you give your judgment for each of the 10 statements.

Do not put your name anywhere on the questionnaire or on any pages you add.

Place your completed questionnaire inside the large envelope and place it in Ms. Carlyle's mailbox no later than October 10.

1. The counselor is always available to work with me within a reasonable time.	SD	D	U	A	SA
2. The counselor rarely wants to work with me.	SD	D	U	A	SA
3. The counselor provides real help to my students.	SD	D	U	A	SA
4. The counselor is unable to help me with instructional problems.	SD	D	U	A	SA
5. The counselor is able to help me with student behavior problems.	SD	D	U	A	SA
6. The counselor gives me the kind of assistance I need.	SD	D	U	A	SA
7. The counselor is never around when I need him.	SD	D	U	A	SA
8. The counselor works with me on solving the problems I bring to him.	SD	D	U	A	SA
9. The counselor knows what my students need to function successfully.	SD	D	U	A	SA
10. The counselor is not effective in the classroom.	SD	D	U	A	SA

Please use the space below to add any comments or suggestions you'd like to make concerning the overall quality of the counseling program at McKinley Elementary School, the strengths and weaknesses of the program, and how the program should be improved. Attach additional pages if needed.

Figure 6.1. Survey Instrument

calculated the percentage corresponding to each number. For example, for Statement 1, the number of teachers who selected each response looked like this:

	SD	D	U	A	SA
1. The counselor is always available to work with me within a reasonable time.	0	2	1	5	8

Determining Percentages of Responses

These results indicated that none of the teachers disagreed strongly with the statement, two disagreed somewhat, one was uncertain, five agreed somewhat, and eight agreed strongly. Each of these response counts was converted to a percentage by first dividing it by the total number of teachers surveyed (16), and then multiplying the resulting fraction by 100. The percentages were rounded to whole numbers to simplify the task of interpretation. For example, the percentage of teachers who disagreed somewhat with Statement 1 was found to be $(2 \div 16) \times 100 = (0.125) \times (100) = 12.5$, which was rounded up to 13%.

When the responses to each statement were analyzed in this way, the results are shown in Table 6.1.

Interpreting Results of the Questionnaires

The questionnaire contained at least one statement designed to assess each of the four dimensions (adjectives) listed in Indicator 9.4. Statement 2 was intended to indicate the counselor's responsiveness. Statements 3, 4, 5, 6, 9, and 10 pertained to the counselor's competence in teacher consultation and classroom guidance. Statements 1 and 7 addressed the counselor's availability. Finally, Statement 8 was designed to indicate the counselor's willingness to work collaboratively.

Examining Results on Individual Items

Because 88% of the teachers marked "strongly disagree" in response to Statement 2 ("The counselor rarely wants to work with me"), the evaluation team concluded that the counselor tended to be responsive to teachers' requests. Similarly, teachers' responses to statements 1 and 7 indicated the counselor was available to teachers when they needed him.

The issue of the counselor's competence was more complex. Although most teachers provided a positive response to Statement 3 ("The counselor provides real help to my students"), noticeable percent-

TABLE 6.1 Results of Survey Questionnaire in Percentages

	SD	D	U	A	SA
1. The counselor is always available to work with me within a reasonable time.	0	13	6	31	50
2. The counselor rarely wants to work with me.	88	6	0	6	0
3. The counselor provides real help to my students.	0	13	19	38	31
4. The counselor is unable to help me with instructional problems.	0	6	6	44	44
5. The counselor is able to help me with student behavior problems.	0	0	0	6	94
6. The counselor gives me the kind of assistance I need.	19	13	13	25	31
7. The counselor is never around when I need him.	94	6	0	0	0
8. The counselor works with me on solving the problems I bring to him.	0	13	13	19	56
9. The counselor knows what my students need to function successfully.	0	13	69	19	0
10. The counselor is not effective in the classroom.	0	6	6	44	44

ages of teachers were either uncertain or slightly negative on this point. The root of this discontent might be found in teachers' responses to Statement 4 ("The counselor is unable to help me with instructional problems"). The survey revealed that 88% of teachers were in agreement with this statement. In contrast, virtually all the teachers agreed with Statement 5 ("The counselor is able to help me with student behavior problems"). The mixed response to Statement 6 ("The counselor gives me the kind of assistance I need") reinforced the earlier indication that the counselor was effective in dealing with some types of problems but ineffective in dealing with others. That 69% of the teachers marked "uncertain" in response to Statement 9 ("The counselor knows what my students need to function successfully") suggested that many teachers did not have a good sense of the counselor's knowledge. Perhaps this statement was inappropriate for the questionnaire, given that teachers could only observe the counselor's behaviors, not his knowledge. Finally, teachers' overwhelming agreement with Statement 10 ("The counselor is not effective in the classroom") was consistent with their earlier suggestion that the counselor was far more effective in consultations about student behavior problems than instructional problems.

On the issue of the counselor's willingness to work collaboratively, teachers' responses to Statement 8 ("The counselor works with me on solving the problems I bring to him"), although positive, indicated less than unanimous agreement.

Communicating Results to the Counselor

Applying the Results and Interpretation

In the spirit of improving the counselor's performance and thereby improving the functioning of the counseling program, Ms. Snow arranged a meeting with the counselor to discuss the results of the survey and to develop an improvement strategy. Emphasizing the positive first, Ms. Snow pointed out the counselor's availability, his willingness to respond to teachers' concerns, and teachers' strong endorsement of his ability to assist them with student behavior problems. The survey results indicated a clear need to increase the counselor's competence in consulting with teachers about instructional problems and in working with students in a classroom setting. To help the counselor develop new skills in these areas, Ms. Snow obtained financial support from the school district's staff development fund to help the counselor take appropriate graduate coursework, one evening per week, at the state university that was an hour from Midville.

The counselor was eager to improve his skills, and the teachers were very pleased that a constructive response to the evaluation had been developed. To help the counselor focus his development, the teachers agreed to meet with him to explain the kinds of instructional problems with which they most needed his help and support.

Summary of Evaluation Principles

This example illustrated several important principles that should be kept in mind in all program evaluations. These principles include the following:

1. Do not attempt to evaluate every aspect of a program at once. Focus the evaluation by selecting a few indicators of quality from the list in Resource A.
2. When choosing a method of data collection, try to select an alternative that minimizes the burden on those who will be asked to provide information.
3. Remember that evaluation often requires hard judgments and negative responses that people might be reluctant to express. If at all possible, design the evaluation in ways that permit those who provide information to preserve their privacy. Always guarantee confidentiality; if possible, provide anonymity.
4. Whenever possible, collect information in ways that give every member of the group of interest an opportunity to respond. Remember that you typically will want to draw conclusions about the judgments of "all teachers", "all parents", or "all students". When the group to be represented is small (say, smaller than 100), collecting information from everyone is better than collecting information

from a sample. It is difficult to obtain a representative sample when the group to be sampled is small.

5. Ask questions your information providers are able to answer, and avoid questions that require speculation. Remember that behaviors can be observed, but judgments concerning knowledge (or attitudes) are speculative.
6. Collect information that will help to identify areas of program success and weakness and will guide remedial action when improvement is needed.
7. Whenever possible, seek redundant information. Ask several questions about each important evaluation issue, and seek information from more than one source. Consistent information from several sources is more trustworthy than information from a single source. Consistent responses to several questions are far more trustworthy than responses to a single question.

Alternative Strategies

Obtaining Supplemental Information

Because Indicator 9.4 was phrased in terms of teachers' beliefs, teachers were the obvious source of information for assessing this indicator. As discussed earlier, the evaluation team considered and rejected the possibilities of collecting judgments from teachers through face-to-face interviews or in a group meeting. The evaluation team also might have gained additional insights by using either of these data collection strategies after the teachers had completed the anonymous questionnaires. Interviews have the advantage of permitting in-depth probing and clarification of initial responses, whereas mailed questionnaires do not.

In this evaluation, it would have been useful to obtain information on the types of instructional help the teachers sought from the counselor and the experiences in which they believed the counselor fell short. Although the planned group meeting between the teachers and the counselor will likely help in this regard, individual interviews might provide more useful information.

Keep in mind that the objective of this evaluation was identification of strengths and weaknesses in the counseling program so that its effectiveness could be improved. Added depth could only help in achieving this objective.

Cautions Regarding Misinterpretation

It would be easy to summarize the results of this evaluation by concluding that McKinley's counselor is a willing worker who makes himself available to teachers, is willing to work collaboratively with teachers, and provides effective consultation regarding student behavior problems but lacks the ability to provide instructional support for teachers. Such a summary is far too glib, however, given the data at hand.

Limitations of the Survey

Because information on each of these dimensions was collected through only one or two questions, the data provided by this evaluation should be regarded as suggestive rather than conclusive. It might not be the case that the counselor lacks ability in responding to instructional problems; this inference is unwarranted in light of the data collected. It might be found, upon further investigation, that the teachers and the counselor communicated in ways that resulted in a lack of understanding of the instructional problems to be addressed.

It is also important to remember that this evaluation sought teachers' perceptions of the counselor's functioning and did not collect data on his actual activities or his effectiveness in helping students. Although teachers' perceptions are critically important, they are not a substitute for information on changes in students' behaviors or abilities that result from the counselor's interventions.

Conclusion

As illustrated in these six vignettes, school personnel can employ relatively simple, straightforward evaluation methods to obtain practical and compelling information about their school counseling programs. Evaluation results can be used to plan a relevant program, enhance specific program activities, document the impact of these activities, and illustrate the need for and effectiveness of the school counseling program.

Effective program evaluation is planned and systematic. School personnel in the six vignettes consistently followed a sequence of tasks: identifying the specific evaluation question(s), choosing a method of collecting information that would answer the question(s), planning and carrying out a systematic procedure for collecting information, organizing the information in a summary format, and interpreting the data summary to provide answers to the evaluation question(s). Such a step-by-step evaluation plan can help ensure that meaningful results, vital to continued support and improvement of school counseling programs, are obtained.

Perhaps the most important messages for readers of this guide are the following:

1. School personnel *can* conduct effective evaluations of their school counseling programs.
2. By conducting program evaluations, school personnel, including counselors, can be convincing advocates for their programs, their students, and themselves.
3. Ongoing evaluations provide vital information to school counselors and other personnel in their continuous efforts to improve school counseling programs.

School counselors often must take the lead in educating their many and varied audiences of teachers, administrators, school board members, parents, and others about the significance of their work. The authors offer this guide to school counselors and other school personnel as a tool toward empowerment. With the knowledge and skills to conceive, design, and conduct program evaluations, school counselors and others interested in school counseling programs can take the wheel of their programs and steer public opinion to obtain the support that is vital to continued growth.

About the Resources

What Is in Resource A

The first column of Resource A consists of standards and indicators for effective school counseling programs. This listing is based on an extensive review of the empirical literature and professional association standards for the field of school counseling (Borders & Drury, 1992). It is intended as a guide for evaluating schools counseling programs.

Because it would be expensive and time-consuming to evaluate every indicator of a standard at the same time, it is suggested that evaluations be narrowed to one indicator. First, locate the heading in capital letters that best describes the general area of interest for an upcoming evaluation. Some areas, such as RESOURCES, have more than one standard, so that a specific standard also must be considered, such as Staffing, Materials, or Facilities.

Once the standard for evaluation has been selected, choose the indicator that seems most appropriate and feasible for your specific evaluation question. For example, assume that you are interested in the standard of Program Evaluation. Is your interest in assessing needs for the expansion of services (Indicator 8.5) or in determining the effectiveness of an existing service (Indicator 8.6)?

The second column of Resource A lists possible evaluation methods that are appropriate to each indicator listed. If you chose Indicator 8.5 for evaluation, then you would find "documentation of needs assessment" in the adjacent column. Several of the evaluation methods listed in the second column are illustrated in the vignettes that constitute the core of this guide. A key to these six vignettes is located in the third column of Resource A. For example, the evaluation method appropriate to Indicator 8.5 (needs assessment) is illustrated in Vignette 1.

What Is in Resource B

Resource B consists of a brief list of references that have been selected to provide the reader with additional examples and explanations of the evaluation methods, procedures, and principles found in this guide. The articles and documents have been organized according to one of three types of evaluation, depending upon the evaluation question under consideration: Needs Assessment, Formative Evaluation, and Summative Evaluation.

Under Needs Assessment, articles and documents illustrate various procedures, methods, measures, and instruments that can be employed in evaluations that ask questions such as the following: What are students' needs for direct counseling services? What are students' needs for classroom guidance? What are teachers' needs for consultation?

Articles and documents in the Formative Evaluation section illustrate procedures, methods, measures, and/or instruments designed to shed light on the following types of evaluation questions: Do program components operate in intended ways? What is the nature of the current program as delivered? What strengths in the current program should be used to greater effect? What weaknesses in the current program should be remedied?

In the Summative Evaluation section, articles and documents illustrate procedures, methods, measures and/or instruments designed to answer such questions as the following: Should this school counseling program be continued? Should the program be replaced? Results and their implications for school counseling programs are discussed.

For an extensive review of the empirical literature and professional standards in the field of school counseling, the reader is referred to the following source:

Borders, L. D., & Drury, S. M. (1992). Comprehensive school counseling programs: A review for policymakers and practitioners. *Journal of Counseling and Development, 70,* 487-498.

Resource A: Standards and Indicators for the Evaluation of School Counseling Programs With Suggested Evaluation Methods and Key to Vignettes

Standards and Indicators	Evaluation Methods	Key to Vignettes
RESOURCES		
Staffing		
Standard 1. School counseling programs are staffed and operated by appropriately trained and qualified personnel.		
1.1. Counselors hold a valid school counselor certificate.	Inspection of personnel records	
1.2. Counselors hold a master's degree from a CACREP-approved program in school counseling or a master's-level school counseling program that included comparable academic and experiential components.	Inspection of personnel records	
1.3. Designated head counselors (department chairs) are certified, experienced counselors who have additional training in administrative and counseling (clinical) supervision skills.	Inspection of personnel records	
1.4. Support personnel (i.e., secretaries, registrars, volunteers) assigned to the school counseling office have been trained appropriately to address the particular functions of the office and the needs of the student population.	Inspection of personnel records	

Standards and Indicators	Evaluation Methods	Key to Vignettes
Standard 2. An adequate number of personnel are available to operate an effective school counseling program.		
2.1. Counselor:student ratios fall within the recommended range of 1:100 to 1:300, based on identified needs of the student body and school community.	Inspection of district records	
2.2. The numbers of support personnel (i.e., secretaries, registrars, volunteers, student assistants) are adequate for fulfilling the functions of the school counseling office and for meeting the specified objectives of the school counseling program.	Interview or survey of counselors	5, 6
2.3. The composition of the school counseling staff is representative of minorities in the school community.	Inspection of district records	
Standard 3. Counselors are involved regularly in a variety of professional development activities.		
3.1. School counselors develop an annual individual professional development plan that includes specific goals, appropriate activities, and indicators of progress; such plans become a part of the performance appraisal process.	Inspection of personnel development records	
3.2. School counselors have access to and participate in a variety of appropriate professional development activities related to identified needs or program objectives.	Survey of counselors, inspection of personnel development records	6
3.3. School counselors receive regular supervision (program and counseling/clinical) from qualified personnel.	Interview or survey of counselors, inspection of counselor logs	5, 6
3.4. School counselors keep current through active involvement in local, state, and national professional organizations (e.g., attending and/or presenting at conventions, reading journals).	Interview or survey of counselors, inspection of personnel development records	5, 6

Facilities

Standard 4. Facilities are adequate, appropriate, and available for all school counseling program activities, allow for the maintenance of confidentiality, and support a student-centered program.

Resource A

Standards and Indicators	Evaluation Methods	Key to Vignettes
4.1. Counselors and support staff have adequate work spaces that allow them to maintain the confidentiality of student information (e.g., records, scheduled appointments, referral slips) and interoffice conversations.	Interview or survey of counselors, inspection of facilities	5,6
4.2. Counselors have regular access to areas that are appropriate for small group counseling and large group guidance.	Interview or survey of counselors, inspection of facilities	5, 6
4.3. The guidance resource center is housed in an area adjacent to the school counseling office and is easily accessible to students, teachers, and parents.	Inspection of facilities	
4.4. Facilities are easily accessible to students, parents, and teachers.	Inspection of facilities	

Materials

Standard 5. Materials, supplies, and equipment are appropriate and sufficient for fully implementing goals of the school counseling program.

5.1. Adequate and appropriate materials, including printed, audio, and video materials, are available.	Interview or survey of counselors, inspection of materials	5, 6
5.2. Adequate and appropriate assessment materials, including a variety of educational, career, and psychosocial instruments, are available.	Interview or survey of counselors, inspection of materials	5, 6
5.3. Technological equipment allows for efficiently completing administrative and clerical tasks.	Interview or survey of counselors, inspection of equipment	5, 6
5.4. Materials are nonbiased (e.g., gender, culture, ethnicity, sexual orientation, disability) in their content and presentation.	Inspection of materials	
5.5. As needed, parallel materials in languages other than English are available.	Inspection of materials	
5.6. Informational materials cover a variety of options and resources that are adequate and appropriate (e.g., full range of post-secondary educational and career opportunities).	Inspection of materials	
5.7. Materials and equipment are current and in good repair.	Interview or survey of counselors, inspection of materials	5, 6

Standards and Indicators	Evaluation Methods	Key to Vignettes

PROGRAM PLAN

Standard 6. The school counseling program is based on a high-quality, comprehensive program plan.

6.1. The program plan includes a philosophy or mission statement.	Inspection of program plan	
6.2. The program plan indicates broad program goals.	Inspection of program plan	
6.3. The program plan includes specific student competencies including those related to career, educational, personal, and social development that are the desired outcomes (operationalized objectives) of the program.	Inspection of program plan	
6.4. Student competency statements reflect the mission statement of the program, are developmentally appropriate, and are measurable.	Inspection of program plan	
6.5. The program plan includes listings of appropriate program activities, materials, and resources (i.e., unit plans, resource or curriculum guides) for addressing program goals and student competency areas.	Inspection of program plan	
6.6. The program plan includes appropriate evaluation criteria and methodology for each program activity, student competency area, and program goal.	Inspection of program plan	
6.7. The program plan indicates prioritized objectives (goals and student competencies) for the current school year, specific activities for addressing these objectives, and methods for evaluating effectiveness.	Inspection of program plan	
6.8. The program plan is based on results of needs assessments, including assessments of students, teachers, parents, community members, employers, and graduates, and on results of program evaluations.	Documentation of needs assessments and previous program evaluations, comparison to program plan	1
6.9. The program plan includes an appropriate balance of individual counseling, group counseling, classroom guidance, and consultation activities, and a comprehensive student advisory system.	Inspection of program plan	

Resource A

Standards and Indicators	Evaluation Methods	Key to Vignettes
6.10. The program plan is revised each year based on results of program evaluations, changes in priorities and needs, changes in professional guidelines, and implications of published research.	Documentation of needed changes, comparison to program plan	1, 2, 3, 4, 5, 6

PROGRAM IMPLEMENTATION

Standard 7. All aspects of the program plan are implemented appropriately and effectively.

Standards and Indicators	Evaluation Methods	Key to Vignettes
7.1. Program implementation adequately reflects the program plan, including the philosophy or mission statement and broad program goals.	Interview of counselors, inspection of records of counseling activities and/or logs	5
7.2. Program implementation activities are related directly to desired outcomes (i.e., student competencies) specified in the program plan.	Interview of counselors, inspection of records of counseling activities and portfolio of counseling materials	5
7.3. Program implementation draws on the activities, materials, and resources specified in the program plan.	Inspection of records of counseling activities and portfolio of counseling materials	
7.4. Program implementation includes appropriate evaluation activities, as specified in the program plan.	Inspection of records of counseling activities and portfolio of counseling materials	
7.5. Program implementation reflects the prioritized objectives (i.e., goals and student competencies), activities, and evaluation methods for the current school year, as specified in the program plan.	Interview of counselors, inspection of records of counseling activities, as compared to program plan	5
7.6. Program implementation provides activities that meet assessed needs of students, teachers, parents, community members, employers, and graduates.	Inspection of records of counseling activities, as compared to results of needs assessments	1
7.7. At least 50% of program activities involve direct contact with students (i.e., individual counseling, group counseling, classroom guidance).	Inspection of records of counseling activities, inspection of counselor logs	
7.8. Specified times are set aside throughout the school year for counselors' individual appointments with students.	Interview of counselors, survey of students, inspection of counselor logs	5, 6

Standards and Indicators	Evaluation Methods	Key to Vignettes
7.9. A variety of small counseling groups is offered during the school year, including support groups and groups aimed at students' assessed needs related to educational, career, personal, and social development.	Inspection of needs assessment results, interview of counselors, inspection of counselor logs and records of counseling activities	1, 6
7.10. Classroom guidance activities, led by counselors and/or teachers, address students' assessed needs related to educational, career, personal, and social development.	Interview or survey of students, inspection of records of counseling activities, as compared to results of needs assessments	5, 6
7.11. Consultation activities that enhance students' development are provided to teachers, administrators, and parents on a regular basis and include individual contacts, in-service training, and workshops.	Interviews or surveys of administrators, parents, and teachers, inspection of counselor logs	5, 6
7.12. Less than 10% of program activities involve coordination tasks.	Inspection of counselor logs	
7.13. The school counseling program provides equitable services to all students.	Interviews or surveys of students, inspection of records of counseling activities or counselor logs	5, 6

PROGRAM EVALUATION

Standard 8. Evaluation of the school counseling program is comprehensive, systematic, and ongoing.

8.1. The evaluation plan is based on program goals and student competencies.	Inspection of evaluation plan	
8.2. The evaluation plan specifies the design and methodology for conducting evaluations, schedules for data collection, and training for data collectors (as appropriate).	Inspection of evaluation plan	
8.3. The evaluation plan includes a variety of appropriate data collection methods, such as opinion surveys, observations, case studies, pretest-posttest comparisons, participant comparisons, goal attainment scaling, and follow-up studies.	Inspection of evaluation plan	
8.4. The evaluation plan includes annual assessment of specific aspects of each program component (with selection based on program priorities), and, every 1 to 3 years, assessment of the overall program.	Inspection of evaluation plan and evaluation results	

Resource A

Standards and Indicators	Evaluation Methods	Key to Vignettes
8.5. Needs assessments of students, parents, teachers, and other school personnel are conducted regularly as a means of identifying local priority needs.	Documentation of needs assessments	1
8.6. Data on the effectiveness of all program activities are collected routinely.	Documentation of evaluation results, including checklists, observations, standardized instruments, interviews, and surveys	2, 3, 4, 5, 6

PROGRAM OUTCOMES

Standard 9. Evaluation results demonstrate the effectiveness of the school counseling program.

9.1. Evaluation results indicate a majority of students achieve program goals and/or meet specified competencies.	Documentation of evaluation results, including checklists, observations, standardized instruments, interviews, and surveys	2, 3, 4, 5, 6
9.2. Evaluation results indicate that a majority of students, parents, teachers, and administrators hold favorable opinions of the school counseling program.	Documentation of evaluation results, including questionnaires, interviews, and surveys	5, 6
9.3. Evaluation results indicate that students believe confidentiality is maintained within specified limits, see counselors as their advocates, and believe counselors are accessible and competent to help them with their educational, career, personal, and social concerns.	Documentation of evaluation results, including questionnaires, interviews, and surveys	5, 6
9.4. Evaluation results indicate that teachers believe counselors are responsive, competent, available, and collaborative.	Documentation of evaluation results, including questionnaires, interviews, and surveys	5, 6
9.5. Evaluation results are used in program revision.	Inspection of program plan	
9.6. As appropriate, summary reports of program evaluation studies are provided to administrators, teachers, parents, and students.	Inspection of reports	

PROGRAM CLIMATE

Standard 10. The atmosphere of the school counseling program is conducive to effective implementation of the program.

10.1. Written policies and procedures exist to protect students' human and civil rights (e.g., access to student records, student referrals, informed consent).	Inspection of written policies	

Standards and Indicators	Evaluation Methods	Key to Vignettes
10.2. Written policies and procedures exist to guide counselors' responses to situations involving emergencies, crisis situations, and situations with legal implications (e.g., suspected child abuse, substance abuse).	Inspection of written policies	
10.3. Administrators are aware of the goals and functions of the school counseling program.	Interview or survey of administrators	5, 6
10.4. School counselors report that administrators allow the appropriate use of counselors' specialized skills and are supportive of school counseling program goals.	Interview or survey of counselors	5, 6
10.5. School counselors report that they are not utilized as administrative assistants nor as disciplinarians.	Interview or survey of counselors	5, 6
10.6. Representatives of the school counseling program staff have regularly scheduled meetings with their principal and district-level administrators to discuss program needs and goals.	Documentation of meetings	
10.7. Administrators and teachers understand and respect the confidential nature of school counseling functions.	Interview or survey of administrators and teachers	5, 6
10.8. The roles and responsibilities of each supervisor of the school counseling program/ staff are stated clearly.	Inspection of role statements	
10.9. School counselors report that the school counseling program is allowed some autonomy in implementing district-level goals and priorities.	Interview or survey of counselors	5, 6
10.10. School counselors report that district-level administrators support the school counseling program through public relations work, funding, and defining appropriate roles and functions.	Interview or survey of counselors	5, 6
10.11. Public relations are an ongoing part of the school counseling program.	Documentation of public relations activities	
10.12. Public relations products emphasize the benefits of the school counseling program and are clear, simple, and positive in their message.	Inspection of public relations products	
10.13. Members of the school-community advisory committee include students, parents, teachers, administrators, and a variety of community representatives.	Documentation of committee membership	

Resource B: Selected References on Program Evaluation

General References for Program Evaluation in Education

These resources define program evaluation terms (e.g., unobtrusive measures) and explain program evaluation procedures (e.g., random sampling). These resources are written clearly and are rich in examples.

Herman, J. L. (Ed.). (1990). *Program evaluation kit.* Newbury Park, CA: Sage.

Jaeger, R. M. (1984). *Sampling in education and the social sciences.* New York: Longman.

Worthen, B. R., & Sanders, J. R. (1987). *Educational evaluation: Alternative approaches and practical guidelines.* New York: Longman.

References for School Counseling Program Evaluation

The articles and documents that follow have been organized according to one of three objectives of evaluation, depending upon the evaluation question under consideration: needs assessment, formative evaluation, and summative evaluation. (See the introductory section of this guide for an explanation of these terms.)

Needs Assessment

The following articles and documents illustrate various procedures, methods, measures, and instruments that can be used in evaluations that ask questions such as the following: What are students' needs for direct counseling services? What are students' needs for classroom guidance? What are teachers' needs for consultation? Many of the articles and documents include the results of needs assessments and discuss how the results can be used. The reader should find the "how to" approaches of these articles and documents easy to read and understand. An asterisk has been placed at the end of references that include samples of the needs assessment instrument(s) used in the evaluation.

Baharoglu, B. J. (1989). Developing and upgrading an elementary and middle school guidance program: A case study. *School Counselor, 37,* 23-37.

Braucht, S., & Weime, B. (1990). Establishing a rural school counseling agenda: A multiagency needs-assessment model. *School Counselor, 37,* 179-183.

Cook, D. W. (1989). Systematic needs assessment: A primer. *Journal of Counseling and Development, 67,* 462-463.

Elliott, S. N., & Gresham, F. M. (1987). Children's social skills: Assessment and classification practices. *Journal of Counseling and Development, 66,* 96-99.

Louisiana State Department of Education, Bureau of Student Services. (1984). *Guidelines and procedures for the design of developmental guidance and counseling programs in Louisiana schools.* Baton Rouge: Author. (ERIC Document Reproduction Service No. ED 262 304)*

Myrick, R. D. (1987). *Developmental guidance and counseling: A practical approach.* Minneapolis, MN: Educational Media Corporation.

New Hampshire Comprehensive Guidance and Counseling Project. (1988). *New Hampshire comprehensive guidance and counseling program: A guide to an approved model for program development.* Plymouth, NH: Plymouth State College. (ERIC Document Reproduction Service No. ED 294 122)*

Oregon State Department of Education. (1984). *Middle school guidance and counseling: Suggested guidelines for school districts.* Salem: Author. (ERIC Document Reproduction Service No. ED 255 838)*

Rimmer, S. M., & Burt, M. A. (1980). Needs assessment: A step-by-step approach. *School Counselor, 28,* 59-62.

Russo, T. J., & Kassera, W. (1989). A comprehensive needs-assessment package for secondary school guidance programs. *School Counselor, 36,* 265-269.

Formative Evaluation

Articles and documents in this section illustrate procedures, methods, measures, and/or instruments designed to shed light on the following types of evaluation questions: Do program components operate in intended ways? What is the nature of the current program as delivered? What strengths in the current program should be used to greater effect? What weaknesses in the current program should be remedied? In many of the articles, implications of the results for school counseling programs are discussed. The reader probably will have minimal difficulty in reading and understanding these articles and documents. An asterisk appears at the end of references that include item or instrument samples.

Baldwin, C. L., Collins, J. R., Kostenbauer, T., & Murphy, C. B. (1988). Research choices for measuring outcome of high school groups. *Journal of Specialists in Group Work, 13,* 2-8.

Bowman, R. P., & Myrick, R. D. (1987). Effects of an elementary school peer facilitator program on children with behavior problems. *School Counselor, 36,* 369-378.

Bundy, M. L., & Boser, J. (1987). Helping latchkey children: A group guidance approach. *School Counselor, 35,* 58-65.

Davis, B., et al. (1987). *Evaluation report of the K-12 comprehensive guidance program of the San Diego City Schools.* San Diego, CA: San Diego City Schools, Planning, Research, and Evaluation Division. (ERIC Document Reproduction Service No. ED 299 498)*

Gerler, E. R., Jr., & Anderson, R. F. (1986). The effects of classroom guidance on children's success in school. *Journal of Counseling and Development, 65,* 78-81.

Hutchinson, R. L., & Bottorff, R. L. (1986). Selected high school counseling services: Student assessment. *School Counselor, 33,* 350-354.

Kerr, B. A., & Ghrist-Priebe, S. L. (1988). Intervention for multipotentiality: Effects of a career counseling laboratory for gifted high school students. *Journal of Counseling and Development, 66,* 366-369.*

Morse, L. A. (1987). Working with young procrastinators: Elementary school students who do not complete school assignments. *Elementary School Guidance and Counseling, 21,* 221-228.

Myrick, R. D., Merhill, H., & Swanson, L. (1986). Changing student attitudes through classroom guidance. *School Counselor, 33,* 244-252.

Omizo, M. M., Hershberger, J. M., & Omizo, S. A. (1988). Teaching children to cope with anger. *Elementary School Guidance and Counseling, 22,* 241-245.

Omizo, M. M., & Omizo, S. A. (1987). Effects of parents' divorce group participation on child-rearing attitudes and children's self-concept. *Journal of Humanistic Education and Development, 25,* 171-179.

Sandler, S. B. (1989). Teaching job search skills to eighth-grade students: A preview of the world of work. *School Counselor, 36,* 219-223.*

Tedder, S. L., Scherman, A., & Wantz, R. A. (1987). Effectiveness of a support group for children of divorce. *Elementary School Guidance and Counseling, 22,* 102-109.

Wiggins, J. D., & Moody, A. H. (1987). Student evaluations of counseling programs: An added dimension. *School Counselor, 34,* 353-361.

Summative Evaluation

The following articles and documents illustrate procedures, methods, measures and/or instruments designed to answer such questions as the following: Should this school counseling program be continued? Should the program be replaced? Results and their implications for school counseling programs are discussed. The interested reader probably will *not* find the majority of these articles difficult to read and understand. An asterisk appears at the end of references that include samples of items or entire instruments.

Boser, J. A., Poppen, W. A., & Thompson, C. L. (1988). Elementary school guidance program evaluation: A reflection of student-counselor ratio. *School Counselor, 36,* 125-135.

Bruckner, S. T., & Thompson, C. L. (1987). Guidance program evaluation: An example. *Elementary School Guidance and Counseling, 21,* 193-196.*

Connor, E. L., & Wasman, M. (1984). *Evaluation of the DCPS Secondary Guidance Program.* Miami, FL: Dade County Public Schools, Office of Educational Accountability. (ERIC Document Reproduction Service No. ED 264 242)*

Gysbers, N. C., & Henderson, P. (1988). *Developing and managing your school guidance program.* Alexandria, VA: American Association for Counseling and Development.*

Helliwell, C. B., & Jones, G. B. (1975). Reality considerations in guidance program evaluation. *Measurement and Evaluation in Guidance, 8,* 155-162.

Jackson, M. D., & Brown, D. (1986). Use of systematic training for effective parenting (STEP) with elementary school parents. *School Counselor, 34,* 100-104.

Kim, S., McLeod, J., & Palmgren, C. L. (1989). The impact of the "I'm special" program on student substance abuse and other related student problem behavior. *Journal of Drug Education, 19,* 83-95.

Murray, P. V., Levitov, J. E., Castenell, L., & Joubert, J. H. (1987). Qualitative evaluation methods applied to a high school counseling center. *Journal of Counseling and Development, 65,* 259-261.

Robie, B. D., Gansneder, B. M., & Van Hoose, W. H. (1979). School guidance and counseling program outcomes and measures for their assessment. *Measurement and Evaluation in Guidance, 12,* 147-165.

Index

Anonymity, 69, 74
Assessment:
  methods and measures:
    face-to-face interviews, 54, 65, 69, 75
    focus groups, 54, 65
    likert scale, 13, 60-61, 65, 70
    needs assessment, 3, 6, 12-19, 30, 80
    observation, 30-42. *See also* Observation
    standardized instrument, 19, 43-52. *See also* Standardized instrument
    structured interview, 19, 53-66, 69. *See also* Structured interview
    survey questionnaire, 11-19, 65, 67-76. *See also* Survey questionnaire
  of classroom guidance, 43-52
  of group counseling, 30-42
  of individual counseling, 20-29
  of parents' opinions, 53-66
  of students' preferences, 2, 11-19
  of teachers' opinions, 67-76
Assignment:
  for observation, 36-37
  to groups, 32-33

Behavior checklist, 21, 26, 27, 33
  administration of, 23
  alternatives to, 27-28
  creation of, 22-23
  limitations of, 28
  rationale for, 22
  utilizing results of, 24-27
Borders, L. D., 5, 79

Career counseling, 2, 43-52
Career Development Inventory, 44-51
Checklists, 22, 27. *See also specific types*
Classroom guidance, 40, 43-52, 68, 69, 84, 85, 86. *See also* Standardized instrument
Confidence limits, 14, 17, 18, 55, 65, 69, 87, 88
Consultation, 68, 69, 84, 85, 86
Control groups, 30-32, 51, 52
  random assignment to, 32-33
  use of, 32
  vs. counseling groups, 39
Correlation, 41

Data:
  analysis of, 8, 15-16
  baseline, 23-24, 25
  collection of, 7, 8, 12-13, 21, 23, 31-32, 44, 68-70, 54-59
    random sample, 8, 12, 18, 55, 59, 75
  interpretation of, 8, 9, 16, 25-27, 49-50, 62-64, 72-74, 139-140
  organization of, 8, 15-16, 24, 37-38, 60-62, 70-72
  reporting of, 9
Difference scores, 37
Drury, S. J., 5, 79

Evaluation:
  focus of, 11-12, 21-22, 31, 43-44, 53-54, 68-69

principles of, 18, 27, 40-41, 50, 64-65, 74-75
team/consultants, 7.
See also Program evaluation

Face-to-face interviews, 54, 65, 69, 75
Focus groups, 19, 54, 65
Formative evaluation, 3, 4, 6, 9, 20-29, 80, 90-91
Frequency distribution, 9

Gain score, 38
Generalization, 18, 19
Goal attainment, 86
Group counseling:
  assessment of preference for, 11-19
  evaluation of, 30-42.
  See also Observation

Individual counseling, 20-29, 68, 84, 85. See also Behavior checklist
Informed consent, 14, 18
Interviews, 7, 8, 19, 54, 69-76
  face-to-face, 54, 65, 69
  structured, 19, 53-66
  training, 34-36, 41, 55, 59, 86

Jaeger, R. M., 55

Likert scale, 13, 60-61, 65, 70

Mean, 9, 37, 46, 48-49, 60, 61, 65

Needs assessment, 2-3, 4, 6, 11-19, 30, 80, 84, 89-90
Norm group, 44, 47, 48-49, 50

Observation:
  alternatives to, 41-42
  assignment of students for, 36-37
  control groups, 32-33, 39
  creation of instrument for, 13, 22-23, 33-36, 69-70

direct vs. indirect, 22, 27-28, 33-37, 86
limitations of, 42
rationale for, 33
standardizing of, 35-36
training observers for, 34-36, 41, 55, 59, 86
utilizing results from, 37-40
Open-ended question, 62, 64, 65

Parent interview. See Structured interview
Percentages, 46, 60, 61, 62, 66, 72, 73
Percentile, 44-45, 46-50
Pilot testing and instrument, 18, 35
Pre-post evaluation, 29, 30-42, 51, 52, 86
Pre-post test, 37, 51-52
Proactive program evaluation, 4, 11-12
Program evaluation:
  focusing, 4, 6, 11-12, 21, 31, 74
  plan, 9, 10, 30
  principles, 18, 27, 40-41, 50-51, 64-65, 74-75
  rationale for, 2-4, 77
  steps in, 77
    analyzing information, 8, 9, 16, 25-27, 49-50, 62-64, 72-74, 139-140
    collecting information, 7, 8, 12-13, 21, 23, 31, 44, 54-59, 68-70
    focusing the evaluation, 6, 7, 11, 21, 31, 43-44, 53-54, 68
    organizing information, 8, 15, 24, 37-38, 60-62, 70-72
    reporting information, 9
  time line for, 8, 9
  types of:
    formative, 3, 9, 21, 80
    needs assessment, 3, 6, 12-19, 30, 80
    summative, 3, 21, 80
Public relations, 54, 88

Quality, indicators of, 4, 7, 12, 21, 29, 31, 44, 54, 68

Random assignment, 32-33, 36-37, 51
  for observation, 36-37
  sampling procedure, 55-59

Index

to groups, 32-33
Rank ordering, 13
Raw scores, 46
Reliability, 44, 45, 51
Reliability, interrater, 35-36, 41
Replication, 28-29
Representativeness, 55, 60
Response format, 70
Response set, 34, 70

School advisory committee, 54
Selection effect, 32
Self report, 41
Small group counseling, 2, 11-19, 21, 30-42, 68, 84, 85
Standard deviation, 46, 48, 49
Standardized administration, 13, 18, 47-51
Standardized assessments, 2, 19, 45, 50
Standardized instrument:
   administration of, 47
   alternatives to, 51
   Career Development Inventory, 45-47
   limitations of, 51
   rationale for, 44-45
   utilizing results of, 48-50
Standardizing:
   observations, 35-36
   questionnaire administration, 13
Standards and indicators, 9, 72, 75, 79
Standard scores, 46-48, 49
Step-by-step program. *See* Systematic program evaluation
Structured interview, 54-66
   alternatives to, 65
   creating the protocol for, 55
   limitations of, 65-66

   rationale for, 53-54
   selection of interviewees, 55-59
   training interviewers, 59
   utilizing results of, 60-64
Student competencies, 12, 18, 31, 44, 45, 49, 51, 54, 84, 85, 86, 87
Student survey. *See* Survey questionnaire
Subscales, 46, 48, 49
Summative evaluation, 3-4, 6, 21, 26, 80, 91-92
Super, 33
Survey questionnaire, 8, 69, 86
   administration of, 13
   alternatives to, 75
   confidentiality, 14
   creation of, 13
   limitations of, 19, 76
   procedures for, 70
   rationale for, 12-13, 69
   utilizing results of, 15-17, 70-74
   writing likert scale items for, 70
Systematic program evaluation, 77, 86

Target behavior, 23, 24, 25
Teacher survey. *See* Survey questionnaire
Test manual, 45, 50

Unobtrusive measures, 27, 51

Validity, 19, 44, 45, 50, 51
Variance, 9, 46
Volunteers, 22, 47, 50, 54, 55, 59

In compliance with GPSR, should you have any concerns about the safety of this product, please advise: International Associates Auditing & Certification Limited The Black Church, St Mary's Place, Dublin 7, D07 P4AX Ireland
EUAR@ie.ia-net.com

www.ingramcontent.com/pod-product-compliance
Lightning Source LLC
Chambersburg PA
CBHW051213290426
44109CB00021B/2442